Finding and Fixing Vulnerabilities in Information Systems

The Vulnerability Assessment & Mitigation Methodology

Philip S. Antón
Robert H. Anderson
Richard Mesic
Michael Scheiern

Prepared for the Defense Advanced Research Projects Agency

RAND
National Defense Research Institute

The research described in this report was sponsored by the Defense Advanced Research Projects Agency. The research was conducted in RAND's National Defense Research Institute, a federally funded research and development center supported by the Office of the Secretary of Defense, the Joint Staff, the unified commands, and the defense agencies under Contract DASW01-01-C-0004.

Library of Congress Cataloging-in-Publication Data

Finding and fixing vulnerabilities in information systems : the vulnerability assessment and mitigation methodology / Philip S. Anton ... [et al.].
p. cm.
"MR-1601."
ISBN 0-8330-3434-0 (pbk.)
1. Computer security. 2. Data protection. 3. Risk assessment. I. Anton, Philip S.

QA76.9.A25F525 2003
005.8—dc21

2003012342

Cover design by Barbara Angell Caslon

Published 2003 by RAND
1700 Main Street, P.O. Box 2138, Santa Monica, CA 90407-2138
1200 South Hayes Street, Arlington, VA 22202-5050
201 North Craig Street, Suite 202, Pittsburgh, PA 15213-1516
RAND URL: http://www.rand.org/
To order RAND documents or to obtain additional information, contact Distribution Services: Telephone: (310) 451-7002; Fax: (310) 451-6915; Email: order@rand.org

PREFACE

Vulnerability assessment methodologies for information systems have been weakest in their ability to guide the evaluator through a determination of the critical vulnerabilities and to identify appropriate security mitigation techniques to consider for these vulnerabilities. The Vulnerability Assessment and Mitigation (VAM) methodology attempts to fill this gap, building on and expanding the earlier RAND methodology used to secure a system's minimum essential information infrastructure (MEII). The VAM methodology uses a relatively comprehensive taxonomy of top-down attributes that lead to vulnerabilities, and it maps these vulnerability attributes to a relatively comprehensive list of mitigation approaches. The breadth of mitigation techniques includes not only the common and direct approaches normally thought of (which may not be under one's purview) but also the range of indirect approaches that can reduce risk. This approach helps the evaluator to think beyond known vulnerabilities and develop a list of current and potential concerns to head off surprise attacks.

This report should be of interest to individuals or teams (either independent of or within the organization under study) involved in assessing and mitigating the risks and vulnerabilities of information systems critical to an organization's functions—including the discovery of vulnerabilities that have not yet been exploited or encountered. The report may also be of interest to persons involved in other aspects of information operations, including exploitation and attack.

This report refers to, in multiple places, a prototype spreadsheet that implements the methodology using Microsoft Excel 2000. Readers may obtain a copy of this spreadsheet online at www.rand.org/publications/MR/MR1601/.

Unpublished RAND research by the authors of this report explored the issues in applying VAM methodology to military tactical information systems. This research may be available to authorized government individuals by contacting Philip Antón (anton@rand.org) or Robert Anderson (anderson@rand.org).

This study was sponsored by the Information Technology Office (ITO) of the Defense Advanced Research Projects Agency (DARPA). It was conducted in the Acquisition and Technology Policy Center of RAND's National Defense Research Institute, a federally funded research and development center (FFRDC) sponsored by the Office of the Secretary of Defense, the Joint Staff, the unified commands, and the defense agencies.

CONTENTS

FIGURES

TABLES

SUMMARY

As information systems become increasingly important to the functions of organizations, security and reliable operation of these systems are also becoming increasingly important. Interoperability, information sharing, collaboration, design imperfections, limitations, and the like lead to vulnerabilities that can endanger information system security and operation. Unfortunately, understanding an organization's reliance on information systems, the vulnerabilities of these systems, and how to mitigate the vulnerabilities has been a daunting challenge, especially for less well-known or even unknown vulnerabilities that do not have a history of being exploited.

RAND has developed and evolved a methodology to help an analyst understand these relationships, facilitate the identification or discovery of system vulnerabilities, and suggest relevant mitigation techniques. This Vulnerability Assessment and Mitigation (VAM) methodology builds on earlier work by Anderson et al. (1999) and fills a much-needed gap in existing approaches by guiding a comprehensive review of vulnerabilities across all aspects of information systems (including not only cyber objects but also physical, human/social, and infrastructure objects[1]) and mapping the vulnerabilities to specific security techniques that can address them.

The VAM methodology takes a top-down approach and seeks to uncover not only vulnerabilities that are known and exploited or revealed today but also the vulnerabilities that exist yet have not been exploited or encountered during operation. Thus, the methodology helps to protect against future threats or system failures while mitigating current and past threats and weaknesses. Also, sophisticated adversaries are always searching for new ways to attack unprotected resources (the "soft underbelly" of the information systems). Thus, the methodology can be valuable as a way to hedge and balance both current and future threats. Also, the complexity of information systems, and their increasing integration with organizational functions, requires additional considerations to ensure that design or architectural weaknesses are mitigated.

[1]An "object" is any part of the system that contributes to the function, execution, or management of the system. The partitioning of information system components into conceptual "objects" facilitates the consideration of components that can otherwise be neglected in security assessments (i.e., security breaches can arise from weaknesses in physical security, human limits and behavior, social engineering, or compromised infrastructure in addition to the more publicized compromises, such as network attacks). It also allows the separation of vulnerability attributes from the system component that may have that attribute.

MAPPING SECURITY NEEDS TO CRITICAL ORGANIZATIONAL FUNCTIONS

The methodology employs the following six steps:

1. Identify your organization's essential information *functions.*
2. Identify essential information *systems* that implement these functions.
3. Identify *vulnerabilities* of these systems.
4. Identify pertinent *security techniques* to mitigate these vulnerabilities.
5. *Select and apply* techniques based on constraints, costs, and benefits.
6. *Test* for robustness and actual feasibilities under threat.

   Repeat steps 3–6 as needed.

The methodology's guiding principles are the links back through critical systems to important organizational functions as well as assessments of the appropriateness of security techniques in each specific situation. This approach not only guides the evaluator through the myriad possible security techniques selections but also provides management rigor, prioritization, and justification for the resources needed, helping others to understand what needs to be done and why.

IDENTIFYING WELL-KNOWN AND NEW VULNERABILITIES

Vulnerabilities arise from the fundamental properties of objects. The VAM methodology exploits this fact to provide a relatively comprehensive taxonomy of properties across all object types, leading the evaluator through the taxonomy by using a table of properties applied to *physical, cyber, human/social,* and *infrastructure* objects (see Table S.1). This approach helps the evaluator avoid merely listing the standard, well-known vulnerabilities (a bottom-up, historical approach), but asks questions outside the range of vulnerabilities commonly identified. For example, vulnerabilities arise not only from such access points as holes in firewalls but also from such behavioral attributes as gullibilities or rigidities. These attributes may be exhibited by all types of system components: cyber, physical, human/social, or infrastructure.

IDENTIFYING AND DOWNSELECTING MITIGATIONS TO IMPLEMENT

The VAM methodology identifies a relatively comprehensive taxonomy of security technique categories to prevent, detect, and mitigate compromises and weaknesses in information systems (see Figure S.1). These techniques are grouped by techniques that improve system *resilience and robustness*; techniques that improve *intelligence, surveillance, and reconnaissance (ISR)* and *self-awareness*; techniques for *counterintelligence* and *denial of ISR and target acquisition*; and techniques for *deterrence and punishment*.

Table S.1
The Vulnerability Matrix

RAND*MR1601-tableS.1*

		Object of Vulnerability			
		Physical	Cyber	Human/Social	Enabling Infrastructure
	Attributes	Hardware (data storage, input/output, clients, servers), network and communications, locality	Software, data, information, knowledge	Staff, command, management, policies, procedures, training, authentication	Ship, building, power, water, air, environment
Design/Architecture	Singularity				
	Uniqueness				
	Centrality				
	Homogeneity				
	Separability				
	Logic/ implementation errors; fallibility				
	Design sensitivity/ fragility/limits/ finiteness				
	Unrecoverability				
Behavior	Behavioral sensitivity/ fragility				
	Malevolence				
	Rigidity				
	Malleability				
	Gullibility/ deceivability/naiveté				
	Complacency				
	Corruptibility/ controllability				
General	Accessible/ detectable/ identifiable/ transparent/ interceptable				
	Hard to manage or control				
	Self unawareness and unpredictability				
	Predictability				

The methodology uses multiple approaches to identify which security techniques should be considered to address the identified vulnerabilities.

First, a matrix maps each vulnerability to security techniques that are either primary or secondary candidates for mitigating the vulnerability. The matrix also cautions when security techniques can incur additional vulnerabilities when they are implemented (see Figures S.2 and S.3). Finally, the matrix notes the cases in which vulnerabilities actually facilitate security techniques, thus resulting in a beneficial side effect.

Second, users will come to this methodology with different intents, responsibilities, and authorities. The methodology reflects this fact by filtering candidate security techniques based on the evaluator's primary job role—operational, development, or policy. The methodology also partitions information system compromises into the fundamental components of an attack or failure: knowledge, access, target vulnerability, non-retribution, and assessment. *Knowledge* of the target system is needed to design and implement the attack. *Access* is needed to collect knowledge and execute an attack on the target vulnerability. Without the core *target vulnerability*, no attack is possible in the first place. *Non-retribution* (or even its first component of non-attribution) is needed to minimize backlash from the operation. Finally, *assessment* of an attack's success is critical when other operations rely on the success of the attack. In the case of a nondeliberate system failure, only the target vulnerability that enables the failure is the critical component.

RANDMR1601-S.1

Resilience/Robustness

- Heterogeneity
- Redundancy
- Centralization
- Decentralization
- VV&A; SW/HW engineering; evaluations; testing
- Control of exposure, access, and output
- Trust learning and enforcement systems
- Non-repudiation
- Hardening
- Fault, uncertainty, validity, and quality tolerance and graceful degradation
- Static resource allocation
- Dynamic resource allocation
- Management
- Threat response structures and plans
- Rapid reconstitution and recovery
- Adaptability and learning
- Immunological defense systems
- Vaccination

ISR and Self-Awareness

- Intelligence operations
- Self-awareness, monitoring, and assessments
- Deception for ISR
- Attack detection, recognition, damage assessment, and forensics (self and foe)

Counterintelligence, Denial of ISR and Target Acquisition

- General counterintelligence
- Deception for CI
- Denial of ISR and target acquisition

Deterrence and Punishment

- Deterrence
- Preventive and retributive Information/military operations
- Criminal and legal penalties and guarantees
- Law enforcement; civil proceedings

Figure S.1—Security Mitigation Techniques

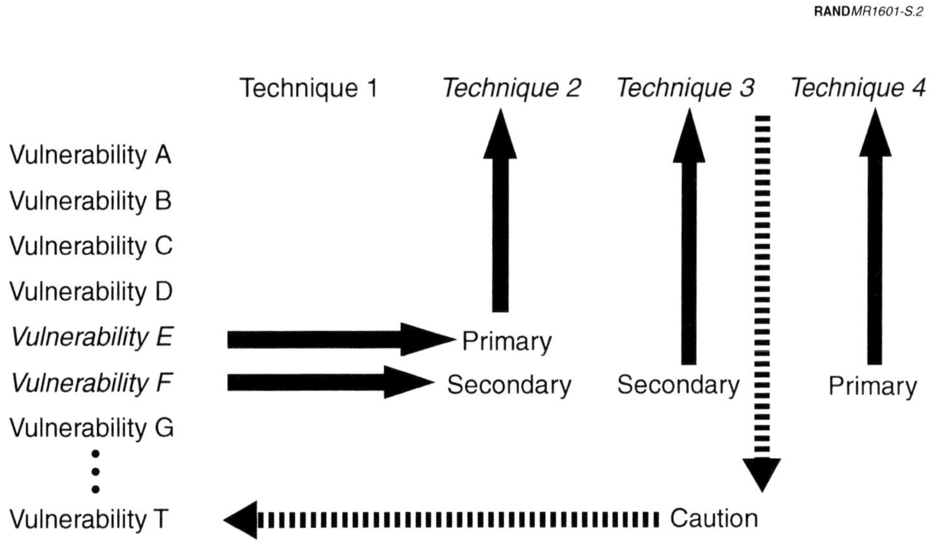

Figure S.2—The Concept of Mapping Vulnerabilities to Security Mitigation Techniques

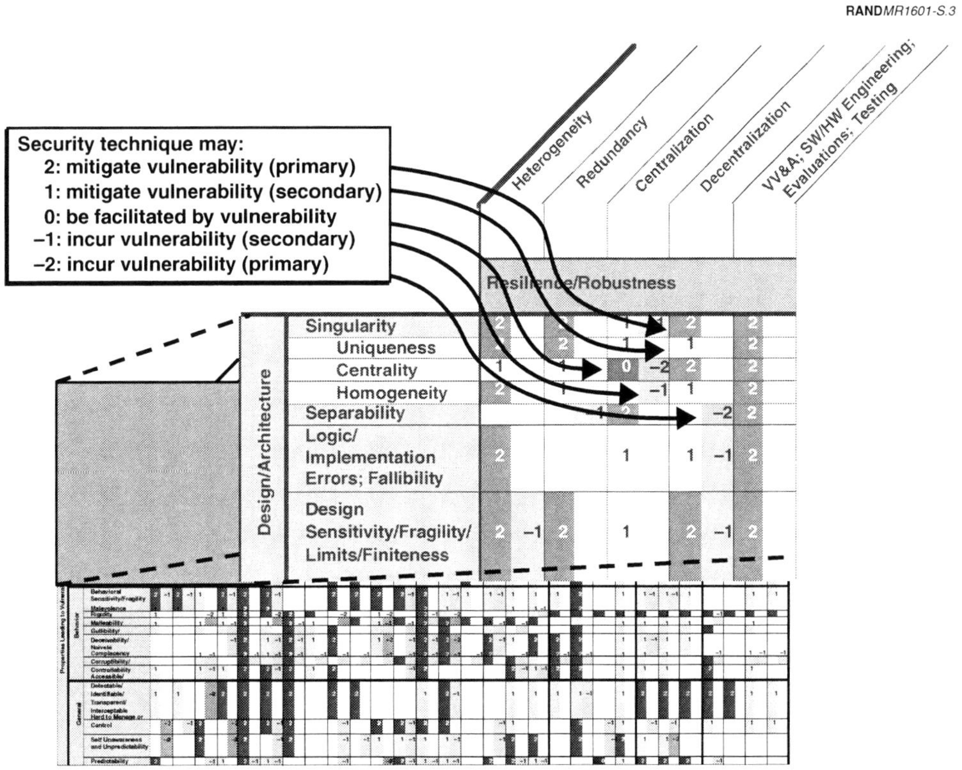

Figure S.3—Values Relating Vulnerabilities to Security Techniques

In addition to filtering the techniques further, this partitioning exploits the important observation that, in attacks, denial of a critical component of an attack can prevent an attack without necessarily addressing the fundamental target vulnerability. The partitioning also suggests additional options for evaluators, based on their situation and job role. For example, operational users cannot redesign the architecture of an information system developed by others, but they can often limit knowledge and access to the system.

AN AUTOMATED AID IN USING THE VAM METHODOLOGY

Finally, an automated prototype tool implemented as an Excel spreadsheet greatly improves the usability of the methodology. The tool guides the evaluator through assessment of vulnerabilities, evaluation of risks, review of cautions and barriers to security techniques, selection of techniques to implement, and estimation of the risks after implementation. Figure S.4 shows the part of the tool where the evaluator specifies his or her job role, and the risks are rated across all five attack components. Readers may obtain a copy of this prototype online at www.rand.org/publications/MR/MR1601/.

RANDMR1601-S.4

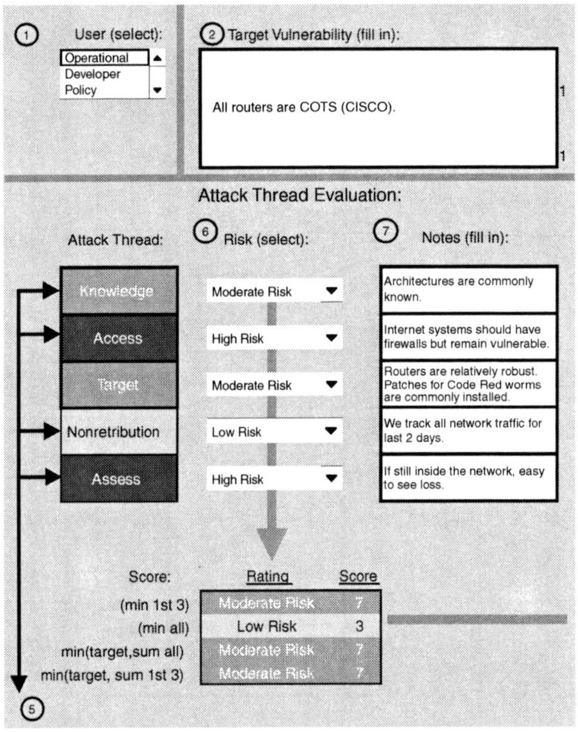

Figure S.4—User and Attack Component Filtering in the VAM Tool (notional values)

CONCLUSIONS

The VAM methodology provides a relatively comprehensive, top-down approach to information system security with its novel assessment and recommendation-generating matrix and filtering methods.

The vulnerabilities and security taxonomies are fairly complete. Viewing vulnerability properties separate from system objects has proved to be a valuable way of reviewing the system for vulnerabilities, since the properties often apply to each type of object. Also, each object type plays an important role in the information systems. The realization and expansion of the vulnerability review to explicitly consider physical, human/social, and infrastructure objects, in addition to cyber and computer hardware objects, recognize and accommodate the importance of all these aspects of information systems to the proper function of these systems.

VAM fills a gap in existing methodologies by providing explicit guidance on finding system vulnerabilities and suggesting relevant mitigations. Filters based on vulnerabilities, evaluator type, and attack component help to improve the usability of the recommendations provided by the methodology.

Providing a computerized aid that executes the methodology during an evaluation greatly improves the usability of the methodology, especially because the current approach generates many more suggestions than the earlier version in Anderson et al. (1999). The current spreadsheet implementation in Excel has the benefit of being usable by the large number of personal computer users who already have the Excel program on their machines. The spreadsheet also gives the user the flexibility to generate analysis reports and even input custom rating algorithms to accommodate local needs and situations.

The methodology should be useful for both individuals and teams. Individuals can focus on their specific situation and areas of responsibility, while teams can bring multiple kinds of expertise to bear on the analyses, as well as perspectives on different divisions within an organization. The methodology also can be used in parallel by different divisions to focus on their own vulnerabilities and can be integrated later at a high-level review once each group's justifications and mappings back to the organization's functions are understood.

ACKNOWLEDGMENTS

Brian Witten of DARPA/ITO proposed examining the utility, completeness, and usability of the earlier published RAND "MEII methodology" for cyber risk assessment by applying it to a real-world Department of Defense critical information system to help validate its usefulness. We appreciate his support and encouragement for this project.

At RAND, we thank Scott Gerwehr for his insights into the use of deception for information security. Robert Drueckhammer provided useful discussions on security practices of computer support departments. MSgt Les Dishman (USAF, on detail to RAND) provided excellent help in obtaining access to needed documents. Finally, we also appreciate the very helpful suggestions, questions, and observations from reviewers Shari Lawrence Pfleeger and Steven Bankes, also of RAND; our report is much better as a result of their thoughtful reviews.

In addition, Claire Antón gave valuable insights into ISO standards and their use.

ATO	air tasking order
C2	command and control
C4I	command, control, communications, computers, and intelligence
CARVER	Criticality, Accessibility, Recuperability, Vulnerability, Effect, and Recognizability
CC	Common Criteria for Information Technology Security Evaluation
CERT	Computer Emergency Response Team
CI	counterintelligence
COTS	commercial off-the-shelf
DARPA	Defense Advanced Research Projects Agency
DDoS	distributed denial-of-service
DoD	Department of Defense
EMP	electromagnetic pulse
GCCS-M	Global Command and Control System–Maritime
I&W	Indications and Warning
I/O	input/output
INFOCON	Information Conditions
IO	information operations
IP	Internet Protocol
ISO	International Standards Organization
ISR	intelligence, surveillance, and reconnaissance
IT	information technology

IVA	Integrated Vulnerability Assessment
IW	information warfare
JFACC	joint force air component commander
LAN	local area network
MEII	minimum essential information infrastructure
MOU	memorandum of understanding
Nmap	Network Mapper
OCTAVE℠	Operationally Critical Threat, Asset, and Vulnerability Evaluation℠
OPSEC	Operations Security
ORM	Operational Risk Management
PKI	public key infrastructure
PP	protection profile
PsyOps	psychological operations
ROM	read-only memory
SIPRNet	Secure Internet Protocol Router Network
SW/HW	software/hardware
TCSEC	Trusted Computer System Evaluation Criteria
USAF	United States Air Force
VAM	Vulnerability Assessment and Mitigation
VV&A	validation, verification, and accreditation

Chapter One

INTRODUCTION

Many organizations' critical functions rely on a core set of information system capabilities. Securing these capabilities against current and future threats requires a broad and unbiased view of system vulnerabilities, as well as creative consideration of security and stability options in the face of resource constraints. Interoperability, information sharing, collaboration, design imperfections, limitations, and the like lead to vulnerabilities that can endanger information system security and operation. Unfortunately, understanding an organization's reliance on information systems, the vulnerabilities of these systems, and how to mitigate the vulnerabilities has been a daunting challenge—especially for less well-known or even unknown vulnerabilities that do not have a history of being exploited.

RAND has developed and evolved a methodology to help analysts understand these relationships, facilitate the identification or discovery of system vulnerabilities, and suggest relevant mitigation techniques. This Vulnerability Assessment and Mitigation (VAM) methodology builds on earlier work by Anderson et al. (1999); it fills a much-needed gap in existing approaches by guiding a comprehensive review of vulnerabilities across all aspects of information systems and mapping the vulnerabilities to specific security techniques that can address them.

The VAM methodology takes a top-down approach and seeks to uncover not only vulnerabilities that are known and exploited or revealed today but also the vulnerabilities that exist yet have not been exploited or encountered during operation. Thus, the methodology helps to protect against future threats or system failures while mitigating current and past threats and weaknesses. Sophisticated adversaries are always searching for new ways to attack unprotected resources (the "soft underbelly" of the information systems); thus, the methodology can be valuable as a way to hedge and balance current and future threats. Also, the complexity of information systems, and their increasing integration with organizational functions, requires additional considerations to ensure that design or architectural weaknesses are mitigated.

WHO SHOULD USE THE VAM METHODOLOGY?

This report should be of interest to individuals or teams conducting vulnerability assessments and planning mitigation responses. Because it facilitates the identification of new vulnerabilities, it should be of particular interest to designers building new systems, as well as to security specialists concerned about highly capable and well-resourced system attackers, such as nation-states or terrorists motivated to identify new security holes and exploit them in subtle and creative ways. The VAM methodology also facilitates a comprehensive review of known vulnerabilities in balance with new vulnerabilities so the user can determine the most serious problems and address them in a rational approach.

The methodology provides a broad view of vulnerability sources (either commonly known or unrecognized until now), system objects, and security alternatives to help avoid prior biases, so both outside assessors and people within an organization should find it useful. However, the methodology requires both objectivity and knowledge of the system in question; therefore outsiders will need access to system experts, while insiders will need to approach an assessment with an open mind.

We also found, in using the methodology to examine operational systems, that people in different roles in an organization have different security options available to them. Thus, designers, operators, and policymakers can all benefit in their complementary use of the methodology.

Furthermore, we found the methodology useful in examining information warfare concepts, in which vulnerabilities and security responses of information systems are important considerations. Thus, the methodology may also be of interest to persons involved in other aspects of information operations (IO), including exploitation and attack.

PREVIOUS RESEARCH

In 1999, Anderson et al. at RAND published *Securing the U.S. Defense Information Infrastructure: A Proposed Approach* (also known as the "MEII Study"). The original goal of the study was to explore the concept of a "minimum essential information infrastructure" (MEII) for the Department of Defense (DoD). The report outlined a six-step process for risk reduction in critical DoD information systems. Its main contribution was a listing of 20 generic areas of potential vulnerability in complex information systems used for command, control (C2) and intelligence. It also listed 13 general areas of security techniques that could be used in various ways to mitigate these vulnerabilities and provided a color-coded matrix showing which security techniques tended to work best against which vulnerabilities. The earlier study's results were theoretical and had not yet been applied to a real system.

In November 2000, Brian Witten of the Defense Advanced Research Projects Agency (DARPA) suggested that the original study's framework should be used to study an operational DoD C2 system to assess the methodology's effectiveness in uncovering unexpected sources of vulnerability and to suggest relevant security techniques for their mitigation. That follow-on study began in spring 2001. This report is one of two documents resulting from that work.

During the course of the study, we determined that the earlier methodology (list of vulnerabilities mapped to a list of security techniques) was valuable; however, the lists needed updating and better ways were needed to handle the large amounts of security suggestions generated. This present report outlines the updated and extended methodology. The VAM methodology now identifies a more comprehensive and taxonomical set of attributes that leads to vulnerabilities and the security techniques that can mitigate them; an expanded map between attributes and security techniques; filters that refine the list of security techniques to consider; and a software tool that automates table and filter lookups, along with additional informational guidance.

Unpublished RAND research by the authors of this report explored the issues and results from applying the VAM methodology to military tactical information systems. Because this study contains details of sensitive information, the results mentioned above may be available only to authorized government individuals by contacting Philip Antón (anton@rand.org) or Robert Anderson (anderson@rand.org). However, the nonsensitive lessons learned from that application study are incorporated in the methodology described below.

STRUCTURE OF THIS REPORT

The rest of this report is organized as follows:

Chapter Two defines what constitutes an information system. It then provides a conceptual discussion of what leads to vulnerabilities and introduces concepts that help to understand vulnerabilities, where they arise, and how they can be mitigated.

Chapter Three provides an overview of the six steps of the VAM methodology along with a notional example. The chapter also describes how the methodology compares with and relates to other security methodologies. Since the core of the VAM methodology involves the identification of vulnerabilities and the selection of security techniques to mitigate them, Chapters Four through Seven provide details of how VAM helps the user accomplish this.

Chapter Four provides an in-depth description of the attributes of system objects that can lead to vulnerabilities (step 3 of the methodology) and examples of how they combine in some well-known information system vulnerabilities.

Chapter Five gives an in-depth description of information system security techniques and examples of how they combine in some well-known security approaches.

Chapter Six describes how the VAM methodology maps the vulnerabilities in Chapter Four to the security techniques in Chapter Five to provide specific guidance on how to address identified vulnerabilities. Next, the chapter illustrates filtering techniques to improve the appropriateness of the security techniques identified in the matrix to the particular user type and attack stage. Chapters Five and Six describe step 4 of the methodology and support the selection of security techniques (step 5). Finally, the chapter provides specific examples of the kinds of specific security countermeasures that can be identified for specific, common information system vulnerabilities by an operational evaluator employing the methodology.

Chapter Seven describes a spreadsheet implementation of the VAM methodology that automates looking up information and explanations in the methodology.

Chapter Eight discusses some deficiencies in the current VAM methodology, possible next steps, and some general discussion.

Chapter Nine presents final conclusions and perspectives.

The Appendix contains detailed information behind the ratings in the matrix that maps vulnerabilities to candidate security techniques.

CONCEPTS AND DEFINITIONS

Before describing the content and processes in the VAM methodology, we need to explore the underlying concepts and terminology it employs: What, for example, constitutes an information system? What leaves such a system vulnerable to attack or failure? What types of components can have vulnerabilities?

SECURITY

"Security" means different things to different people, depending on their view of what can lead to a compromise of the system in question. We take a broad view of security to include any issue that affects the safe and reliable performance of the system. Compromises to the system can therefore arise not only from overt attacks by adversaries but also from accidents, faults, failures, limitations, and natural causes.

INFORMATION SYSTEMS

We use the term "information system" quite broadly to include any system or component (whether physical, cyber, virtual, computer, communication, human, or social) that is involved in storing, processing, handling, or transmitting information. While the scope of an information processing system can be defined more narrowly (i.e., purely by computer software and hardware), we are often concerned with the information-related functions of and for organizations. Anything that can lead to failure in, or compromise of, an information system component can endanger the performance of the organization and its mission, thus imploring consideration when securing the system.

SYSTEM OBJECT TYPES

We explicitly represent the different types of system components according to whether they are physical, cyber, human/social, or enabling infrastructure.

Physical. These objects include, for example, hardware (e.g., data storage, input/output [I/O], clients, and servers), networks and communications between and within nodes, and physical locations at various levels within the system's architecture.

Cyber. Cyber objects include, for example, software, data, information, and knowledge. Often they exist "virtually" in electronic or even conceptual representations that are far removed from the physical forms or media (e.g., disks, paper, binary switches) in which they exist.

Human/Social. Human and social objects include, for example, users and other staff, developers, management, command structures, policies, procedures, training, and authentication.

Enabling Infrastructure. Infrastructures include, for example, physical housings (e.g., buildings, vehicles), power, water, air, and other environmental conditionings.

The scope of this object list allows a more comprehensive examination of all the objects in a system, not merely the computer hardware and software (which are so often focused on). For example, information is processed and handled by humans within an organization, not just by computers and networks. In fact, human processing of information is a key component in information systems, and the vulnerability of human and social systems must be addressed during a comprehensive evaluation of risks.

On the Use of the "Object" Concept

The use of an "object" is a common theoretical tool in information science that allows one to address a person, place, or thing while elucidating its properties or behaviors of interest. The partitioning of information system components into conceptual "objects" allows us to emphasize components that are often neglected when considering security. *Cyber* objects are automated, computerized, software, or virtual components that are normally considered as the components of information systems. However, these objects usually occupy and rely on *physical* objects as well (e.g., the physical devices that instantiate virtual objects, the buildings in which the devices reside, or the physical spectra that they exploit). *Human beings* are other "objects" that process information in the system; they use, manage, and control the system, its objects, and its goals. Humans exist in multiple *social* structures that influence their behavior. Finally, all three of these types of objects rely on *infrastructure* components that are not formally part of the information system yet supply vital support to the system (e.g., power, air, food, temperature control).

ATTRIBUTES AS SOURCES OF VULNERABILITIES

Vulnerabilities arise from identifiable *attributes* of information system *objects*. The VAM methodology explores this genesis explicitly, providing a relatively comprehensive, high-level review of vulnerabilities from first principles and mapping them across all object types. This approach guides the evaluator to examine all vulnerabilities—not just the ones that are known or have been exploited to date—and explores the vulnerabilities across all the system's objects—not just the cyber-related components.

Anderson et al. (1999) first explored the concept of information system vulnerabilities arising from attributes of the information system. Our work builds on these concepts by explicitly separating the objects from the attributes they exhibit and expanding the list of attributes that lead to vulnerabilities.

Separating vulnerability attributes from system object types encourages the examination of potential vulnerabilities from applying attributes normally associated with certain object types to other types of objects in the system. For example, singularities can be present not only in cyber software or physical hardware but also in unique, irreplaceable people (users) who alone know how to operate certain equipment or process certain types of information.

Security Techniques

Finally, we handle the vast number of security techniques in use or under research by the information security community by categorizing them according to the approach they take to mitigate vulnerabilities. Thus, we can methodologically treat these techniques in the abstract and describe how they relate to the vulnerabilities they mitigate. Techniques in each category are listed in Chapter Five. The categories are not of equal size; historically, more attention has been paid to some techniques than to others. In some cases, this skew is quite logical; in other cases, there are new techniques that provide important promise and deserve added attention in the future. Considering the techniques by approach type helps in looking for the best technique that logically meets a vulnerability challenge, without getting unduly distracted by their differences.

Chapter Three

VAM METHODOLOGY AND OTHER DoD PRACTICES IN RISK ASSESSMENT

OVERVIEW OF THE VAM METHODOLOGY

In the late 1990s, RAND published a six-step methodology to improve the security posture of critical information systems (Anderson et al., 1999). The steps were to

1. Identify your organization's essential information *functions.*
2. Identify information *systems* essential to implementing the essential functions in step 1.
3. Identify *vulnerabilities* of the essential systems in step 2.
4. Identify pertinent *security techniques* to mitigate the vulnerabilities in step 3 using the *VAM matching matrix tool.*
5. *Select and apply* techniques from step 4 based on constraints, costs, and benefits.
6. *Test* the techniques applied in step 5 for robustness and actual feasibilities under threat.

   Repeat steps 3–6 as needed.

Note in particular that the methodology includes an explicit mapping of vulnerabilities to security techniques (step 4). This mapping forms the core of the methodology and provides the evaluator with explicit guidance on addressing the vulnerabilities. The current work in this report expands the size and complexity of this matrix to improve the comprehensiveness of the matrix approach.

We give an overview below of how this six-step process works, along with a conceptual military example of its use. Even though we illustrate the basic steps using a military example, the VAM methodology can be applied to other critical commercial and government functions as well.

The most involved parts of the VAM methodology are found in steps 3 and 4 (the identification of vulnerabilities and the generation of security techniques to mitigate them). Chapters Four through Seven provide additional details on the steps beyond what is included here.

Step 1. Identify Essential Information Functions

Information systems are not ends in themselves. They are employed by individuals and organizations to support specific functions and operations. Given limited resources, security vulnerabilities that endanger the *essential* information-based functions should be addressed first. Thus, an individual trying to identify and mitigate these vulnerabilities first needs to distinguish what the essential functions are.

Process. An objective process can guide the identification of an organization's essential information functions.

First, a *strategies-to-tasks* analysis (Lewis and Roll, 1993; Thaler, 1993; Kent and Simons, 1994) can be conducted. Here the goals and strategies of the organization are identified and prioritized, and the strategies are mapped to the tasks (functions) designed to implement the strategies.

Second, specific information functions in support of these tasks are identified and categorized.

Third, *measures of essentiality* are developed and employed to rank the information functions into the following categories: essential, valuable, and expendable. *Essential* functions are those that, if compromised, prevent the organization from performing its important tasks satisfactorily (as defined by the strategy-to-tasks requirements). *Valuable* functions are those in which work-arounds can be identified; yet the work-arounds have significant performance costs and risks. *Expendable* functions are those in which work-arounds with acceptable performance costs and risks can be identified.

Finally, all the identified functions are integrated to develop an overall ranking of information functions. Special attention should be paid to looking for functions essential or valuable to many or all tasks. Also, sets or logical groupings of functions that support numerous tasks should be identified where possible, thus identifying regions of functionality that require particular attention.

Example. In an example of notionally applying the methodology to a military organization, a joint force air component commander (JFACC)[1] performs a number of functions in the execution of an air campaign, including generating and distributing an air tasking order (ATO),[2] analyzing logistics support needs, planning fuel resource allocations, planning medical operations, and teleconferencing with other military

---

[1]DoD defines a JFACC as

> The commander within a unified command, subordinate unified command, or joint task force responsible to the establishing commander for making recommendations on the proper employment of assigned, attached, and/or made available for tasking air forces; planning and coordinating air operations; or accomplishing such operational missions as may be assigned. The joint force air component commander is given the authority necessary to accomplish missions and tasks assigned by the establishing commander. . . . (Joint Chiefs of Staff [2003])

See also Joint Chiefs of Staff (1994) for details on the roles of the JFACC in military air planning.

[2]During military operations, an ATO specifies which aircraft are assigned which tasks (e.g., conducting patrols, dropping munitions on specific targets, providing troop and supply transport).

planners (see Figure 3.1). Of all the functions listed, the generation and distribution of the ATO (in the solid oval) could arguably be selected as the critical function that must be supported in the near term. The other functions are less time-critical and serve secondary support to the generation (and ultimately execution) of the ATO. Thus, we select the generation and distribution of the ATO as the "essential information function" for the JFACC organization.

Step 2. Identify Essential Information Systems

Given the essential information-related functions from step 1, the essential information systems that support or implement these functions now need to be identified.

Process. First, the information systems used to perform the essential functions identified in step 1 need to be identified and categorized. These systems form the list of candidate "essential" information systems.

Again, *measures of essentiality* are developed and employed to rank the information systems as *essential, valuable,* or *expendable.* Finally, all the identified systems are integrated across the functions to develop an overall ranking of information systems. Special attention should be paid to looking for systems critical to many or all functions. Also, sets or logical groupings of systems that support numerous functions should be identified where possible, thus identifying logical sets of systems that require particular attention.

Example. In our continuing example, if located on a ship, a JFACC and his or her staff employ a number of information systems to support their operations. These information systems include the Global Command and Control System–Maritime (GCCS-M), the Global Combat Support System (GCSS) for logistics, the so-called Common Operating Environment (COE) supplied on many general-purpose military computers, the Secure Internet Protocol Router Network (SIPRNet), and the public switched

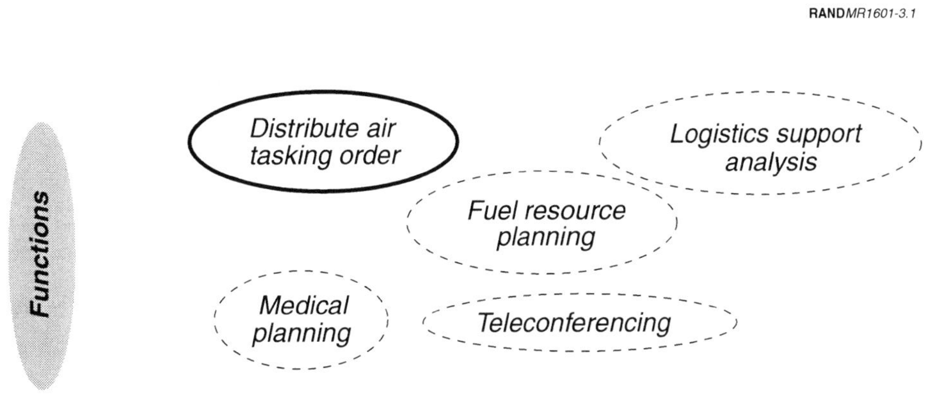

Figure 3.1—Example Functional Decomposition of JFACC Information Functions

telephone network (see Figure 3.2). Because step 1 identified the generation and dissemination of an ATO as the essential function, we need to select the essential information systems that support that function. GCCS-M and SIPRNet (in solid, bold boxes) are the essential information systems that support the ATO. Of these two systems, and from the perspective of passing information to the JFACC for processing, SIPRNet could be identified as the main information communication backbone that is most essential to support the ATO generation and dissemination function; yet GCCS-M is also essential for rapid ATO generation.

Step 3. Identify System Vulnerabilities

Given the prioritized list of essential information systems from step 2, we can now focus on examining the systems for vulnerabilities. This is the step in which the VAM methodology uniquely begins to contribute advice, since many other methodologies lack specific help in determining vulnerabilities. Note that a successful vulnerability assessment requires the insights and experience of system users and developers as outlined below; so both methodological guidance and experience are important.

Here we describe the process involved in step 3, along with a notional example. Chapter Four details how this assessment is conducted from an objective, top-down

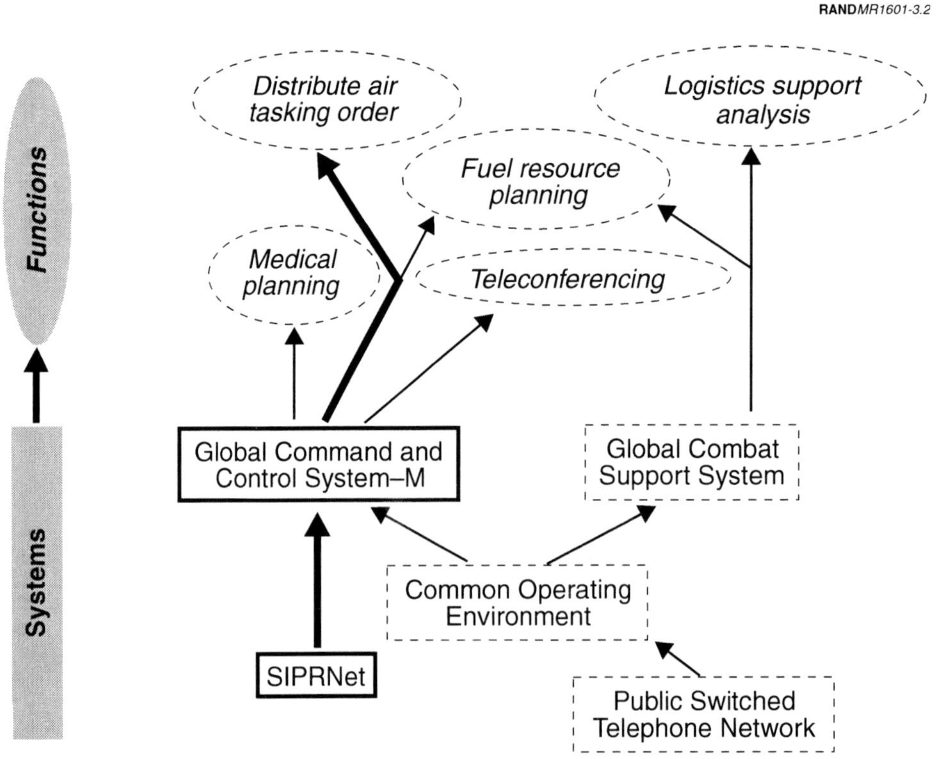

Figure 3.2—Example Information Systems Supporting the JFACC Information Functions

perspective of inherent attributes that lead to vulnerabilities, including additional details on the vulnerability form, specific vulnerability attributes, and the distinction of attributes from system object types. Specific examples of common vulnerabilities are included in Chapter Four and at the end of Chapter Six.

Process. The VAM methodology takes a broad approach to vulnerability analysis by asking the evaluator to complete a matrix containing a relatively comprehensive taxonomy of attributes that lead to vulnerabilities across all types of system objects (see the schematic in Table 3.1).

Vulnerabilities should be reviewed at various levels within a system. For example, a cyber object's vulnerabilities should be reviewed at the global architecture level (e.g., major systems, their interactions, and the systems that provide global communication of data); application components in the architecture (i.e., specific applications ranging from commercial software components to custom applications designed to meet the unique processing needs of the organization's users); common supporting software (e.g., database software, encryption/decryption packages, support libraries); communication-level components (e.g., software that interfaces directly with communication lines), and so on. The goal is to review the components that are key to the system's proper and reliable operation no matter what the level, yet

Table 3.1

Vulnerability Matrix: Attributes of Information System Objects

RANDMR1601table-3.1

		System Objects			
		Physical	Cyber	Human/Social	Infrastructure
Vulnerability Attributes	Design/ Architectural				
	Behavioral				
	General				

judgments of the criticality are important lest the user get buried in noncritical details.

Along with the vulnerability taxonomy, the evaluator should review past experience with the critical systems, asking the following questions:

- What has failed in the past? Why?
- What has been the effect of these failures?
- What corrective actions have been tried?

Efforts should be made to explain these experiences with theoretical models.[3] If the experiences are consistent with the models, then the evaluator should gather statistics on the failures to help identify which have been more serious in the past. If the models are insufficient, then the evaluator should attempt to refine or extend the models or find other models that may help to reveal the underlying reasons why failures have been occurring. These models need not be detailed, but they should help to identify which vulnerability attributes have been leading to failure and which are present in the system.

The evaluator can also look for vulnerabilities by examining the security techniques already employed in the system and considering the vulnerability cautions identified in the matrix in step 4 below associated with these security techniques.

Finally, the evaluator needs to assess what theoretical vulnerabilities are in the system for which there is no real-world or test experience. The evaluator should review the system's components, with the full list of vulnerability attributes, as a checklist. The presence of such attributes represents a potential vulnerability that needs to be investigated further to determine how serious the vulnerability may be. Again, theoretical models of system function may be useful to explore and explain the role these attributes may play in potential compromises or failures. Statistics may or may not be available, but the space of plausible threats or failures should be examined to assess the significance of the potential vulnerability against important capabilities of the information system.

Example. Considering GCCS-M and SIPRNet, identified in step 2, we ask what the critical vulnerabilities are that we need to address to support these information systems (see Figure 3.3). Identification of specific vulnerabilities for these military systems is beyond the scope of this report, so we treat vulnerabilities in the abstract. Notionally, we work through the potential types of vulnerabilities and identify that GCCS-M contains vulnerabilities *E* and *F*. If security technique *3* is already employed in GCCS-M, the user then should also see if vulnerability *T* is present (see Figure 3.4). Remember that we need to search for these vulnerabilities at the various levels of

---

[3]For example, some intrusion detection systems use models of "normal" communication behavior to look for such outliers as heavy communication from a particular piece of software or machine that has historically had very low communication. Other models may be as simple as anticipated component failure rate curves against which data can be collected to locate abnormal failure rates. Still other models may be security profile models of staff that can be used in background checks to help identify possible staff compromises or behavior patterns that may lead to weaknesses and problem behavior.

GCCS-M; so, we should examine GCCS-M as a whole, its primary applications, and the critical supporting components (e.g., SIPRNet). Within SIPRNet, various levels need examination, including the government and commercial software used, the communication systems, the networking system and routers, the administrative operators, and the physical components, such as cabling and critical supporting infrastructure.

Step 4. Identify Pertinent Security Techniques from Candidates Given by the VAM Methodology

Identifying vulnerabilities can be a difficult task, but determining how to address them can be even more difficult and frustrating. The VAM methodology provides a theoretical mapping not only to help prioritize the mitigation techniques that naturally come to mind but also to provide a relatively comprehensive review of other techniques that may not be obvious initially.

Process. The VAM methodology contains a large matrix that identifies general security techniques relevant to each vulnerability. The matrix also identifies cautions where the security technique might incur an additional vulnerability. A schematic of the matrix is included in the example below, illustrating how the matrix is used to identify potential security techniques that address the vulnerabilities of concern.

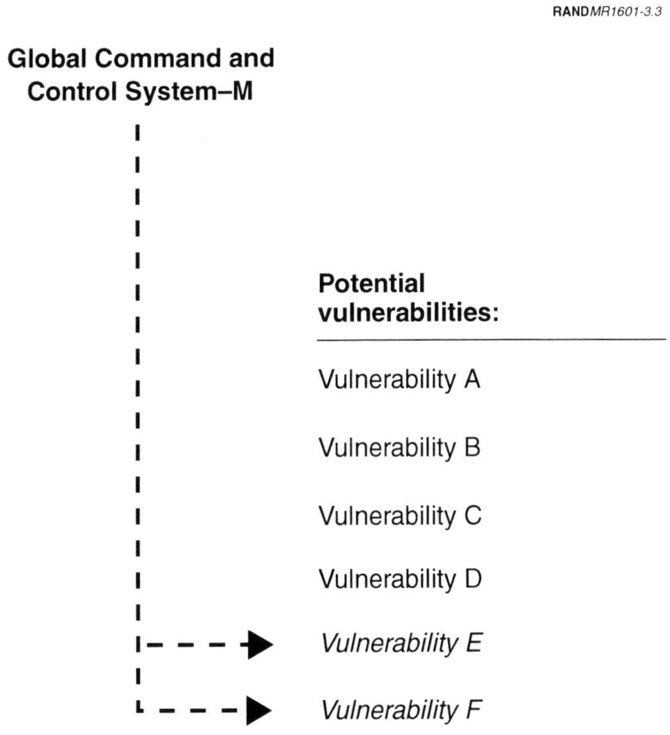

Figure 3.3—Identifying Which Vulnerabilities Apply to the Critical System

Chapters Six and Seven describe this matrix in detail, along with usability issues and a spreadsheet implementation that automates the security technique candidate lookups.

Example. In step 3, vulnerabilities *E* and *F* were identified as the critical notional vulnerabilities for GCCS-M. Figure 3.4 gives a notional diagram of the VAM table that maps these vulnerabilities to appropriate mitigation techniques. In our example, techniques *2* and *4* are the *primary* techniques that may address vulnerabilities *E* and *F* (respectively). Techniques *2* and *3* are alternates, *secondary* techniques that may address vulnerability *F*. Thus, we examine techniques *2* and *4* first to see if they fit the needs of GCCS-M. If they do not, we then consider technique *3*.

The map also identifies vulnerability side effects that may be incurred from the employment of a mitigation technique. Here, technique *3* may introduce vulnerability *T* in some cases, so a *caution* is noted to watch for the incursion of vulnerability *T* if technique *3* is implemented.

Since this example is quite notional, the reader may wish to see the end of Chapter Six for concrete examples of security techniques developed for some common information system vulnerabilities.

Step 5. Select and Apply Security Techniques

Process. The list of appropriate security techniques identified in step 4 must now be culled down to a set that can be implemented given the available resources and responsibilities of the evaluator's organization. While the evaluator can apply some techniques directly, other techniques may be out of the purview of the evaluator and

RANDMR1601-3.4

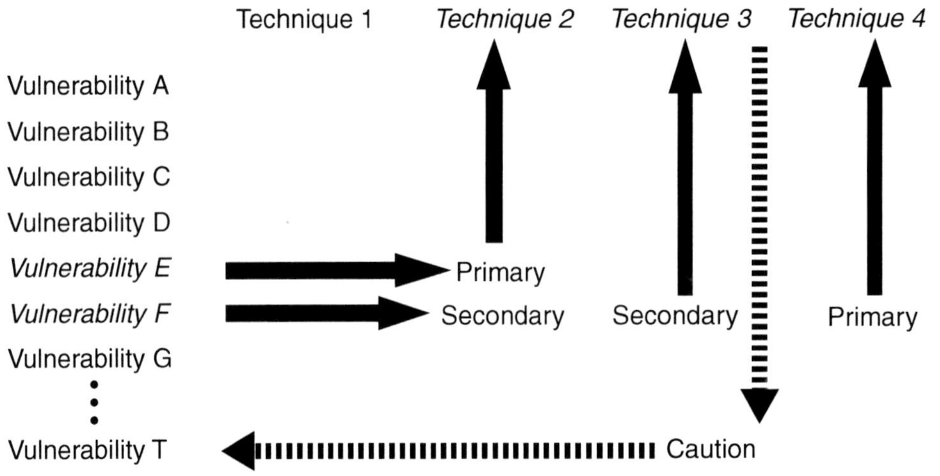

Figure 3.4—The Concept of Mapping Vulnerabilities to Security Mitigation Techniques

his or her organization. In the latter case, promising approaches in this category can be passed along to responsible parties. Also, the large number of options generated by the matrix can suggest other areas that may not have been the most obvious or direct, yet that may reduce the vulnerability of the system. For example, management, counterintelligence (CI), and retribution measures can help protect the system and deter attacks when software changes and protection programs are not options to user communities.

Example. In the example case of GCCS-M, we then apply techniques *2*, *3*, and *4* to bolster GCCS-M (see Figure 3.5).

Step 6. Test for Robustness Under Threat

Simply adding more security techniques does not necessarily imply that the problems have been resolved. The improved system should be tested under actual or simulated threat conditions to determine how effective the mitigation has been. Vulnerability information from such testing can be applied back into step 3 to help determine other security options to consider and apply.

Process. Test the effectiveness of the improved system. *Red teaming* is an important approach for such testing because it provides an independent examination of vulnerabilities and robustness. These teams should not only test against known problems and fixes but also look for and identify new problems (including any introduced inadvertently with the newly added security techniques). Residual concerns should be addressed in realistic exercises (or sometimes in operational settings if appropriate) to test procedures and work-arounds.

Other test approaches may also be useful. The security implementers (or independent parties or companies) that specialize in security assessments could also conduct

RANDMR1601-3.5

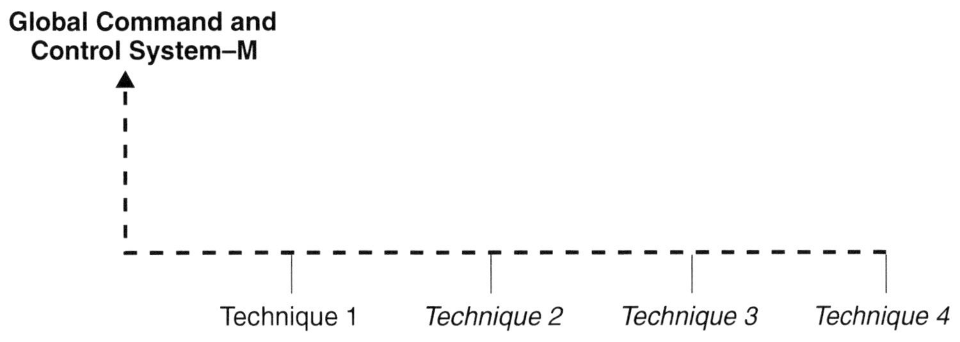

Figure 3.5—Identifying Security Techniques to Consider

an inspection and validation of the implementation. If failure or compromise statistics were utilized in step 3, these values could be compared with post-implementation statistics over a sufficiently long or utilized period to quantify the success of the mitigations. In some cyber parts of the system, automated attack or usage tools could be implemented to explore how well the system responds under simulated attacks. Note, however, that many automated tools are limited to common, well-known, and previously exploited vulnerabilities. Thus, they do not in general address the full breadth of system components, especially when physical, human/social, and infrastructure components are not stressed.

The best test procedures will incorporate a model of the threat to assess the probability of the threat successfully compromising the system. These models should be broad enough to incorporate both the threat's ability to discover a previously unexploited vulnerability and the threat's technical ability to exploit the vulnerability.

The tests may focus on the part of the system that has been modified, but secondary and tertiary effects on the rest of the system and other functions need consideration.

Finally, the results of the tests, along with the previous five steps, should be documented and assessed to determine if additional work is needed starting with step 3.

Example. In our example, a (simulated) threat is applied to GCCS-M to ascertain its robustness (see Figure 3.6).

OTHER DoD VULNERABILITY ASSESSMENT METHODOLOGIES

Many methodologies and assessment techniques are used by the commercial sector and by DoD to identify vulnerabilities and design security activities. We describe briefly some of the more common ones below and discuss how the VAM methodology relates to them.

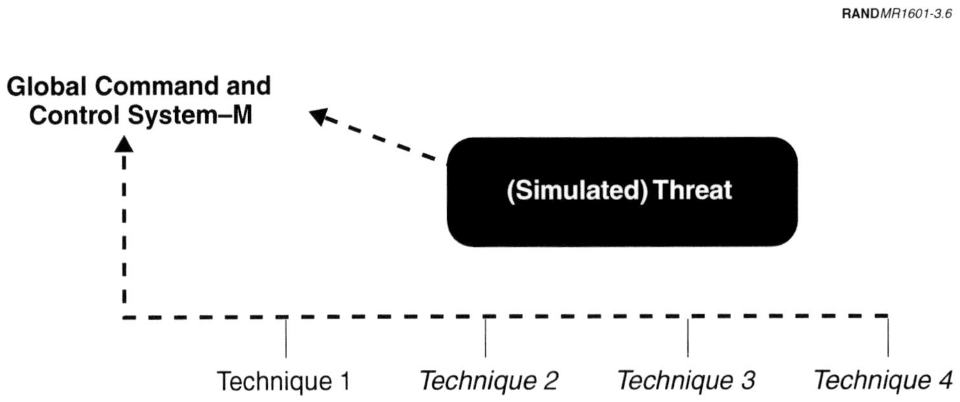

Figure 3.6—Test the Revised System Against (Simulated) Threats

OCTAVE

The Operationally Critical Threat, Asset, and Vulnerability Evaluation^{SM} (OCTAVE^{SM}) is a framework created by the Software Engineering Institute at Carnegie Mellon University for identifying and managing information security risks (Alberts et al., 1999, 2001).[4] It defines a set of processes for identifying important organizational missions, threats to organizations, and vulnerabilities that the threats may exploit. OCTAVE also includes processes for developing protection strategies to reduce the risks from these vulnerabilities and threats. The framework is laid out in the following set of "Processes" (see Alberts et al., 1999):

1. Identify enterprise knowledge.
2. Identify operational area knowledge.
3. Identify staff knowledge.
4. Establish security requirements.
5. Map high-priority information assets to information infrastructure.
6. Perform infrastructure vulnerability evaluation.
7. Conduct multidimensional risk analysis.
8. Develop protection strategy.

OCTAVE is heavily process oriented, helping an evaluator structure a project to analyze and mitigate information security risks. These process guidelines can play a valuable role in organizing the activity, but processes 6 and 8 do not have a system for reviewing the fundamentals that lead to vulnerabilities. Also, these processes do not produce recommended protection strategies relevant to the identified vulnerabilities. Thus, the VAM methodology complements the OCTAVE framework. An evaluator may benefit from the combined use of both approaches.

ISO/IEC 15408: Common Criteria

International Standard 15408, the Common Criteria for Information Technology Security Evaluation (or "CC" for short), is a guideline that indicates which system aspects should be addressed in which categories of processes when evaluating the security of information technology (IT) products and systems.[5,6] The CC is meant to be relevant for "consumers," "developers," and "evaluators" of information systems and components. The CC states that any security analysis should examine the physi-

---

[4] Also see the OCTAVE website at www.cert.org/octave/.

[5] See www.commoncriteria.org for details on the standard and its history.

[6] CC evolved from the Trusted Computer System Evaluation Criteria (TCSEC) developed in the United States in the 1980s. In the early 1990s, Europe developed the Information Technology Security Evaluation Criteria (ITSEC) built on the concepts of the TCSEC. In 1990, the International Standards Organization (ISO; www.iso.ch) sought to develop a set of international standard evaluation criteria for general use. The CC project was started in 1993 to bring all these (and other) efforts together into a single international standard for IT security evaluation. ISO formally accepted CC as International Standard 15408 in 1999.

cal environment a system will exist in, the assets requiring protection, and the purpose of the system to be evaluated ("target system"). It then mandates a listing of the assumptions, threats, and organizational security policies, leading to a set of security objectives to be met. Using these objectives, a set of security requirements should be generated, including functional and assurance requirements as well as requirements for the environment within which the target system will operate. Requirements that recur in various systems and settings become the "protection profile" (PP), which is intended to be reusable and defines the target system's security requirements "known to be useful and effective in meeting the identified objectives, both for functions and assurance. The PP also contains the rationale for security objectives and security requirements."[7] Evaluations—including various types of penetration testing—should then be carried out to determine a level of compliance with the PP.

The CC guidelines are complex, embodying many hundreds of pages of documentation. Much of the vulnerability analysis within the process is based on the *developer's* vulnerability analysis, which is then examined by an *evaluator* to determine completeness and whether "appropriate measures are in place to prevent the exploitation of obvious vulnerabilities in the intended environment."[8] Other tables and charts allow an evaluator to calculate the "attack potential" of a target system based on the elapsed time it would take to perform a successful attack, the expertise required, the knowledge of the target system available, the access required, and the equipment needed.

We cannot do justice here to the CC framework, nor is it our intent to critique it. We do not find within the published materials, however, much guidance for developers and others regarding *where* within the complex architecture of an information system one should look for potential vulnerabilities, *how* to look for them in a methodological way, and *which* security techniques are most applicable in mitigating any flaws found. We believe the concepts and listings in the VAM methodology could be a useful augmentation to the CC process in all these areas.

ISO/IEC 17799: Code of Practice for Information Security Management

International Standard 17799[9] arose from the British Standard 7799 on information security management. It is increasingly used as a substantial checklist for ensuring that information security practices are in place within an organization. It covers many relevant aspects for information security management, including the following:

- security policy (in a documented form)
- organization security (within the organization, the security of third-party access, and security of outsourcing procedures)

---

[7]See Common Criteria (1999a, p. 28).

[8]See Common Criteria (1999e, p. 365).

[9]First edition dated December 12, 2000.

- asset classification and control
- personnel security, including appropriate job definitions, user training, and response procedures
- physical and environmental security
- communications and operations management
- access controls, including monitoring system access and use and security of mobile computing (e.g., wireless) access
- systems development and maintenance
- compliance procedures.

The thoroughness of this set of categories is admirable, but each is treated quite superficially within the standard itself. The checklist within the standard is a reminder of "best practices" resulting from experience with secure/insecure information systems, but the standard does not give much guidance in understanding the levels of threats faced and where vulnerabilities may lurk, which are the underlying motivations for this guidance. We have used the list of security management techniques in this standard as one of the sources consulted in developing our list of security mitigation techniques (see Chapter Five).

Operations Security

Operations Security (OPSEC) as a methodology originated during the Vietnam War as a way of finding out how the enemy was obtaining advanced information on certain combat operations in Southeast Asia.[10] OPSEC is a countermeasures program for protecting critical information (see also Army Regulation 530-1, *Operations Security*;[11] *Joint Doctrine for Operations Security*;[12] Williams, 1999; and Hamby, 2002). OPSEC involves the following five steps:

1. Identify the critical information to be protected.
2. Analyze the threats.
3. Analyze vulnerabilities.
4. Assess risks.
5. Apply countermeasures.

The five OPSEC steps parallel VAM in general, with the added explicit representation of threat and risk assessments. Nevertheless, OPSEC doctrine typically contains little guidance on how to identify vulnerabilities or select countermeasures to address them. Here the techniques in the VAM methodology could be useful.

---

[10]See U.S. Army Communications Electronics Command (1999).

[11]U.S. Department of the Army (1995).

[12]Joint Chiefs of Staff (1997).

Operational Risk Management

Operational Risk Management (ORM) is another military process for managing risks across all hazards facing the military (i.e., including but not limited to information system hazards).[13] ORM is a decisionmaking process designed to review and anticipate basic aspects of hazards and reduce risks to acceptable levels. ORM grew out of ideas originally developed to improve safety in the development of weapons, aircraft and space vehicles, and nuclear power. The U.S. Army adapted ORM in 1991 to reduce training and combat losses. ORM involves the following five steps:

1. Identify hazards.
2. Assess hazards.
3. Make risk decisions.
4. Implement controls.
5. Supervise.

The basic concept in ORM is to conduct a risk-reduction review and provide these five general steps as items that should be considered, rather than providing a detailed methodology for all types of hazards. ORM recommends the use of techniques, such as brainstorming, to generate ideas and affinity diagrams to break down an operation into categories (e.g., enemy, troops, terrain, time) in order to focus the analysis on one area at a time.[14]

As with OPSEC, the five ORM steps parallel VAM in general, with the added explicit representation of making risk decisions. ORM doctrine also contains little guidance on how to identify hazards (vulnerabilities) or select controls (countermeasures) to address them. Here also the techniques in the VAM methodology could be useful.

Integrated Vulnerability Assessments

Navy Integrated Vulnerability Assessments (IVAs) involve checklist reviews of systems in order to list the top vulnerabilities a command is concerned with and is followed by brainstorming security mitigations that can be implemented in response. An additional methodology, CARVER (Criticality, Accessibility, Recuperability, Vulnerability, Effect, and Recognizability), is mentioned as a means for prioritizing vulnerabilities. CARVER uses very rough rating categories that can in themselves be interesting. However, the numeric ratings, and especially the technique of summing these ratings together into a single numeric rating, are flawed. CARVER's simple numeric scoring scheme does not accurately preserve important distinctions among categories. Also, there is little reason to believe that combining ratings of very different aspects of the problem (e.g., time, importance, physical measures, effects) will yield a meaningful numeric score.

---

[13]See, for example, U.S. Department of the Air Force (2000a,b,c); U.S. Naval Safety Center (1997); and U.S. Naval Safety Center, "Operational Risk Management" (webpage).

[14]See, for example, the tutorial by the U.S. Naval Safety Center (n.d.).

Despite the problems with CARVER, the following basic steps of an IVA remain valid:

1. Identify vulnerabilities.
2. Prioritize vulnerabilities.
3. Brainstorm countermeasures.
4. Assess risks.

As with OPSEC and ORM, basic steps in CARVER parallel VAM in general, with the added explicit representation of risk assessments. CARVER contains little guidance on how to identify vulnerabilities, and "brainstorming" countermeasures are of little help. Thus, the techniques in the VAM methodology for identifying vulnerabilities and exploring countermeasures are relevant to CARVER studies.

The VAM Methodology Techniques Fill Critical Needs in Other Methodologies

While many of these methodologies (including VAM) use similar philosophies and guidelines (i.e., reviewing critical functions, identifying vulnerabilities, choosing mitigation techniques, implementing techniques, and testing for robustness under threats), the VAM methodology complements the others in that it provides an explicit mechanism to help an evaluator understand what leads to vulnerabilities, what security techniques apply to the vulnerabilities identified, and what potential problems may arise from the security techniques themselves. Given the good efforts by these organizations to institutionalize security reviews, it may make sense for the organizations to adopt the methods in steps 3 and 4 of the VAM methodology as a way to improve their own utility and provide detailed guidance to the evaluators in their communities (see Figure 3.7).

RANDMR1601-3.7

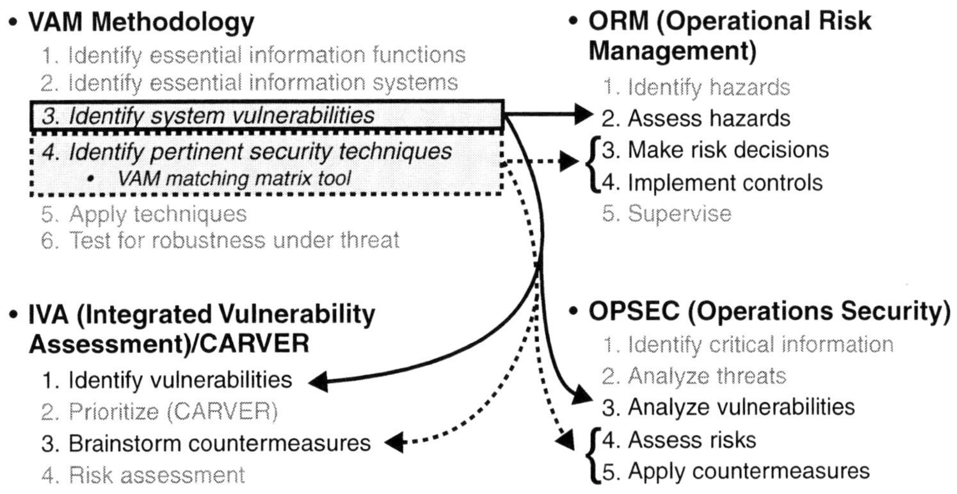

Figure 3.7—The Core of the VAM Methodology Can Be Used in Other Traditional Methodologies

Chapter Four

VULNERABILITY ATTRIBUTES OF SYSTEM OBJECTS

Here we present the lists and descriptions of vulnerability attributes, how they can be mapped in a user form to system objects, and how some common security problems exploit these attributes. Thus, this chapter provides details on step 3 of the VAM methodology.

VULNERABILITY ATTRIBUTE CATEGORIES

Figure 4.1 lists the general properties of objects that can lead to vulnerabilities. Vulnerability attributes include those related to the design and architecture of the system, the behavior and actions taken by the system, and general attributes that cut across both structure and behavior. These somewhat conceptual attributes apply generally to many types of systems and at various levels within the systems.

Table 4.1 maps the attributes that can lead to vulnerabilities to all four types of system objects: physical, cyber, human/social, and supporting infrastructure. Attributes are grouped according to whether they arise from the *design or architecture* of the system object, from the *behavior* of the system object, or more generally from both.

A VULNERABILITY CHECKLIST AND EXAMPLE

Table 4.1 can be used as a checklist or form to be completed by the evaluator when examining the information system. In this way, he or she can review the entire list of vulnerability attributes across all the object types for the system (or subsystem) being studied. Table 4.2 shows the checklist completed with the following common security concerns.

Insider Threat

Vulnerability Attribute: Malevolence.

Type of Target: Human/social.

Description: It is widely believed that the "insider threat" (malevolent behavior by a trusted person with approved access to critical information systems) is the greatest threat to the security of information systems. The "insider" might be someone with a grudge, or co-opted by an enemy through blackmail, bribes, or the like.

RANDMR1601-4.1

Design/Architecture

- Singularity
  - Uniqueness
  - Centrality
  - Homogeneity
- Separability
- Logic/implementation errors; fallibility
- Design sensitivity, fragility, limits, finiteness
- Unrecoverability

Behavioral

- Behavioral sensitivity/ fragility
- Malevolence
- Rigidity
- Malleability
- Gullibility, deceivability, naiveté
- Complacency
- Corruptibility, controllability

General

- Accessible, detectable, identifiable, transparent, interceptable
- Hard to manage or control
- Self-unawareness and unpredictability
- Predictability

Figure 4.1—Properties Leading to Vulnerabilities

Inability to Handle Distributed Denial-of-Service Attacks

Vulnerability Attribute: Behavioral sensitivity/fragility.

Type of Target: Cyber.

Description: One of the most difficult kinds of cyber attacks to handle is the distributed denial-of-service (DDoS) attack, wherein hundreds or thousands of different computers bombard a specific network node or component with packets or requests for service—usually ones with erroneous information that require additional time for processing. Information networks must be specially configured and designed if they are to thwart (to the extent possible) this kind of attack that depends on behavioral characteristics and sensitivities of the network(s).

IP Spoofing

Vulnerability Attribute: Gullibility/deceivability/naiveté.

Type of Target: Cyber.

Description: To "spoof" an Internet Protocol (IP) address, within a packet or message, means to substitute an erroneous address in the place where a valid one should appear. By this means, it becomes difficult to ascertain the true sender of an information packet or session, and therefore to permit various forms of attack that disguise their source.

Table 4.1
Matrix of Vulnerability Attributes and System Object Types

RANDMR1601-table4.1

		Object of Vulnerability			
		Physical	Cyber	Human/Social	Enabling Infrastructure
	Attributes	Hardware (data storage, input/output, clients, servers), network and communications, locality	Software, data, information, knowledge	Staff, command, management, policies, procedures, training, authentication	Ship, building, power, water, air, environment
Design/Architecture	Singularity				
	Uniqueness				
	Centrality				
	Homogeneity				
	Separability				
	Logic/ implementation errors; fallibility				
	Design sensitivity/ fragility/limits/ finiteness				
	Unrecoverability				
Behavior	Behavioral sensitivity/ fragility				
	Malevolence				
	Rigidity				
	Malleability				
	Gullibility/ deceivability/naiveté				
	Complacency				
	Corruptibility/ controllability				
General	Accessible/ detectable/ identifiable/ transparent/ interceptable				
	Hard to manage or control				
	Self-unawareness and unpredictability				
	Predictability				

Table 4.2
Example Completed Vulnerability Checklist

RANDMR1601-table4.2

		Object of Vulnerability			
		Physical	Cyber	Human/Social	Enabling Infrastructure
	Attributes	Hardware (data storage, input/output, clients, servers), network and communications, locality	Software, data, information, knowledge	Staff, command, management, policies, procedures, training, authentication	Ship, building, power, water, air, environment
Design/Architecture	Singularity				
	Uniqueness				
	Centrality	Centralized Network Operations Centers (NOCs)			
	Homogeneity		Standardized software		
	Separability				
	Logic/ implementation errors; fallibility		Weaknesses in router or desktop applications software		
	Design sensitivity/ fragility/limits/ finiteness	Electronic environmental tolerances			
	Unrecoverability				
Behavior	Behavioral sensitivity/ fragility		Inability to handle (DoS) attacks		
	Malevolence			Insider threat	
	Rigidity				
	Malleability				
	Gullibility/ deceivability/naiveté		IP spoofing		
	Complacency				
	Corruptibility/ controllability				
General	Accessible/ detectable/ identifiable/ transparent/ interceptable				
	Hard to manage or control				
	Self-unawareness and unpredictability		Inability to detect changes to IP net, making IP masking possible		
	Predictability	Common commercial hardware is well known and predictable	Common commercial software is well known and predictable		

Inability to Detect Changes to IP Net, Making IP Masking Possible

Vulnerability Attribute: Self-unawareness and unpredictability.

Type of Target: Cyber.

Description: If an IP network does not have active monitoring programs and tools to allow personnel to ascertain whether or not a new host (IP address) has been inserted, or removed, from the net, then it could be possible for someone to insert an unauthorized laptop or another device onto a network connection and download information into that device. This danger is especially prevalent for wireless networks, where the "connection" can be from a location away from visible network ports or even outside the organization's building. This is a lack of "self-awareness" of the network configuration, and changes to it, during its operation.

Centralized Network Operations Centers

Vulnerability Attribute: Centrality.

Type of Target: Physical.

Description: Network operations centers can contain many vital physical components (e.g., key equipment and backups) in one central location. As such, a physical attack could disable not only primary, but also backup, routers and key communications equipment.

Common Commercial Software and Hardware Are Well Known and Predictable

Vulnerability Attribute: Predictability.

Type of Target: Physical and Cyber.

Description: The personal computers, workstations, routers, servers, and other components of critical information systems are often based heavily on commercial products, such as Cisco router software, Windows NT, and Microsoft Outlook, Word, Excel, PowerPoint, etc. As such, the vulnerabilities, organization, and, in some cases, source code of these types of programs are widely known. The programs are thus highly predictable in that other copies of them can be tested to find situations (e.g., exceeding the capacity of a database) in which their performance fails.

Standardized Software

Vulnerability Attribute: Homogeneity.

Type of Target: Cyber.

Description: The heavy use of standardized software for routers (e.g., Cisco operating system), servers (e.g., Windows NT), and PCs/workstations (e.g., Windows NT or Macintosh OS) creates a very homogeneous information and communication system. Any flaw in one of these designs can be replicated widely within the information system and therefore can provide a common vulnerability across the system.

Weaknesses in Router or Desktop Applications Software

Vulnerability Attribute: Logic/implementation errors; fallibility.

Type of Target: Cyber.

Description: There may be fundamental design or implementation flaws in standard software used in operating systems (workstation and router) and desktop applications. These flaws, if they become known to an attacker, could provide unauthorized access or destruction.

Electronic Environmental Tolerances

Vulnerability Attribute: Design sensitivity/fragility/limits /finiteness.

Type of Target: Physical.

Description: Various commercial electronic equipment vital to network communications and computing are often not hardened for environmental influences (e.g., temperature, smoke, humidity) or extreme attack means (e.g., electromagnetic pulses [EMPs]).

DESCRIPTION OF VULNERABILITY ATTRIBUTES

Here are the attributes that lead to vulnerabilities, with short descriptions for each. Additional examples and discussions of these attributes can be found in Anderson et al. (1999).

Note that some vulnerabilities display more than one of these attributes at a time, often leading to a chain of attack or a series of faults to meet the ultimate goal of an attack or resulting in a non-intentional system failure.

Design and Architecture Attributes

The attributes of the design and architecture of a system object provide structural characteristics that can lead to vulnerabilities. These attributes are grouped in the following broad categories:

Singularity. Singularity is an important, broad category that can provide important targets or single points-of-failure with profound effects. Singularity encompasses uniqueness, centrality, and homogeneity.

- ***Uniqueness.*** Uniqueness is *singularity in availability* where an object may be the only one of its kind. Besides being difficult to replace, unique objects may be less likely to have been thoroughly tested and perfected. Examples include one-of-a-kind items no longer being manufactured or people with special knowledge or expertise that cannot be readily transferred to others.
- ***Centrality.*** Centrality is *singularity in location* where the failure points are collected in a single place. Examples include decisions, data, or control passing through a central node or process.
- ***Homogeneity.*** Homogeneity is *singularity in type* where, through replication, multiple, identical objects share common flaws or weaknesses. Using a single type of object provides a common target that, if compromised, affects all the system functions it supports.

Grouping these three types under "singularity" recognizes that these attributes all exhibit singularity but in different ways. For example, a single point of failure may be due to the difficulty in replacing it (uniqueness), the collection of critical nodes in a single location (centrality), or the widespread compromise of a system once the weaknesses in a common object are discovered.

Separability. Separability implies that the object could easily be isolated from the rest of the system. Separable objects are subject to divide-and-conquer attacks, where protection information (e.g., security updates), attack reinforcements, or postattack repairs can be blocked or seriously delayed. Examples include networks that can be bifurcated into two noncommunicating subnets.

Logic and Implementation Errors; Fallibility. Errors in the logic, implementation, or structures of the system object can directly provide access, an exploitable target, or non-attribution to an attacker. These errors can affect system reliability, availability, understandability, maintainability, and other important aspects. Errors and fallibilities can arise from failures to meet system requirements or, in more fundamental flaws, in the requirements themselves. Errors and fallibilities can also arise from insufficient validation, verification, and accreditation (VV&A); insufficient test and evaluation; lack of rigorous systems engineering; or from technical or scientific deficiencies or immaturities.

Design Sensitivity, Fragility, Limits, or Finiteness. Rather than flaws or errors, these attributes arise from the natural limitations of all systems. No real-world system can be designed with unlimited capacity and capability. Examples include vulnerability to environmental exposures, variations in inputs, abnormal use, and overloading. Appropriate error handling could mitigate these limitations, but vulnerabilities ensue when proper error handling is not implemented.

Unrecoverability. Objects that have irreplaceable components or information, as well as those that require an inordinate time (relative to functional requirements) or effort (relative to available resource) to recover from failure states or be replaced, can provide a tempting target if they provide critical capabilities. Examples include systems with long reboot times relative to operational response times and systems that lose critical state information.

Behavioral Attributes

In addition to its structural features, an object's behavior can exhibit characteristics that are exploitable. Here are the major behavioral attributes that can lead to such vulnerabilities.

Behavioral Sensitivity or Fragility. These attributes involve how the object behaves or reacts, and how robust the object is to changes in input and environmental conditions. Examples include behavioral, functional, and operational sensitivity to actions, configurations, settings, inputs, etc.

Malevolence. Systems or people that actively work against the broader information system and its security (e.g., insider threats) can directly damage the function of the system or be exploited by external entities to increase their malevolence.

Rigidity. Rigidity or lack of adaptiveness involves configurations, behaviors, or responses not easily changed in response to an attack. Also, a lack of preplanned procedures (e.g., contingency plans and MOUs[1]) can limit the available actions of an object, making it more likely to fail or greatly slowing its function.

Malleability. Objects that can be easily modified, manipulated, changed, inserted, or deleted pose potential weaknesses to both internal and external threats.

Gullibility, Deceivability, or Naiveté. Objects with these attributes are easy to fool. Examples include recruitable insiders, the inability to handle uncertain data, insufficient trust models, the inability to recognize one's own biases and when they can lead to duping, repudiation and lack of authentication, and the ability to be duped into an inappropriate response (i.e., being manipulated into a security state or posture that is too high or low given the real threat, resulting respectively in less-effective operations or insufficient protections).

Complacency. A lack of security diligence (e.g., poor administrative procedures or insufficient screening) or responsiveness implies a weak security posture and an inability to respond to threats.

Corruptibility or Controllability. These attributes imply a weakness that can be exploited to make an object act in error or become a malevolent agent. Examples include people that can be manipulated or corrupted into insider threats; inputs, outputs, and memory that can be changed; and systems or organizations that can be controlled without the knowledge of their individual components.

General Attributes

These attributes cut across both the structure and behavior of the object.

---

[1]Memoranda of understanding (MOUs).

Accessible, Detectable, Identifiable, Transparent, or Interceptable. These exposures apply to architecture, behavior, adaptations, data, etc., and form the basis of a critical step in an attack. Without access, for example, one cannot attack a system.

Hard to Manage or Control. Difficulty in configuring, controlling, or maintaining an object or system can make it difficult to find, fix, or prevent flaws; establish proper security protections and responses; and bound the behavior of the system or its components.

Self-Unawareness and Unpredictability. Just as knowledge is critical to an attacker, self-awareness is critical to the defender to know who and what constitutes the system, how it interconnects and interoperates, and how and when the system is being compromised. Likewise, the inability to predict how your system is configured or will behave limits the knowledge available to respond to problems and attacks. Self-unawareness can also occur within the system itself (e.g., an inability to detect "alien" code within its own software).

Predictability. Predictability of the object's design, architecture, or behavior by an adversary allows the adversary to plan and construct attacks from afar, to understand how the object will respond, and to manipulate the object into desired states or failure modes.

HOW VULNERABILITY PROPERTIES COMBINE IN COMMON THREATS

The following examples demonstrate how vulnerability properties can be combined to provide significant information security problems.

First, consider DDoS attacks that take down an Internet service by flooding it with seemingly legitimate service requests from multiple, distributed sources. Figure 4.2 shows that DDoS exploits design limits in traffic capacity, rigidity in rerouting and blocking incoming traffic, and difficulty in managing a system in which control is distributed among multiple cooperating entities with no single management authority that regulates traffic.

Second, consider penetrations of firewalls set up to block illegitimate, untrusted, or unauthorized accesses and requests. Figure 4.3 shows that firewall penetrations can take advantage of homogeneity in the global sense that market dominance and standardization in firewalls, routers, and other network components make it easier to exploit known vulnerabilities in these components. Also, when an attacker determines how to penetrate an organization with common firewalls, the attacker can penetrate systems across the entire organization. Firewall penetrations also depend on accessibility vulnerabilities (e.g., presence on open networks), difficulty in firewall and network management (e.g., difficulties in configuring the firewalls initially or in reconfiguring the firewall to block known attackers), and self-unawareness (i.e., when system operators do not know if their systems have been compromised, who the penetrators are, what areas have been compromised, or even how their system is configured so they can adjust the configuration to block further penetrations).

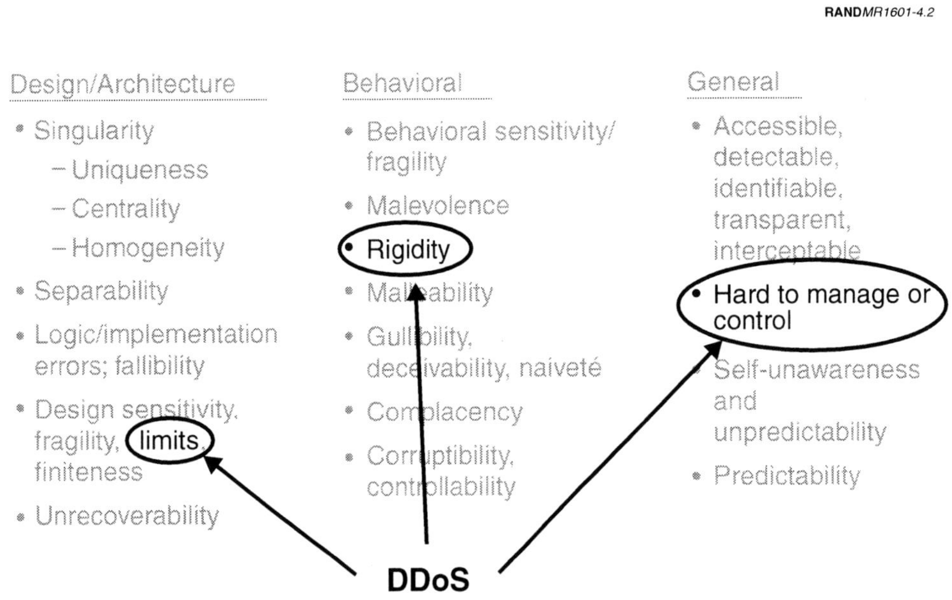

Figure 4.2—Vulnerabilities Enabling Distributed Denial of Service

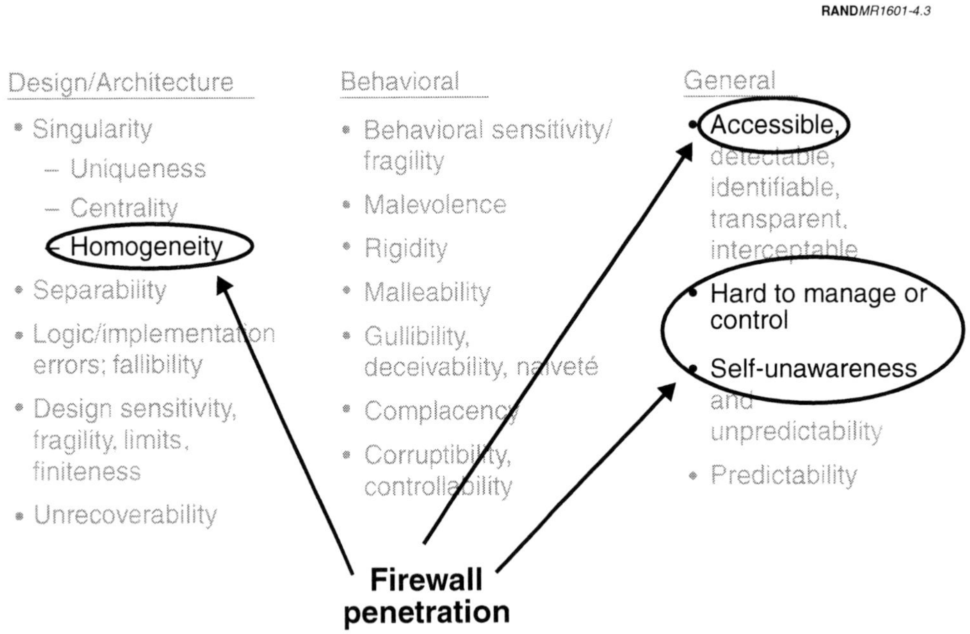

Figure 4.3—Vulnerabilities Enabling Firewall Penetrations

Third, consider network mapping (e.g., using network scanning and probing tools) by an adversary to collect knowledge about the target system for future exploitation. Figure 4.4 shows that network mapping can take advantage of a large number of vulnerabilities. Centrality provides "one-stop shopping" for information, making it easier to find all the systems of interest. Homogeneity implies that the attacker can apply his or her knowledge across a large number of systems or even across the whole organization. Rigidity keeps the network configuration very consistent, preserving the validity of whatever knowledge the adversary gathers. Gullibility allows the network mapper to employ deceptions to gather information (both from cyber probes and from social engineering). Access to the system facilitates probes, open-source intelligence gathering, and social engineering. Difficulty in managing a network, along with unawareness, reduces the ability of the defender to keep out network probes and recognize when one's system is the target of intelligence gathering.

RANDMR1601-4.4

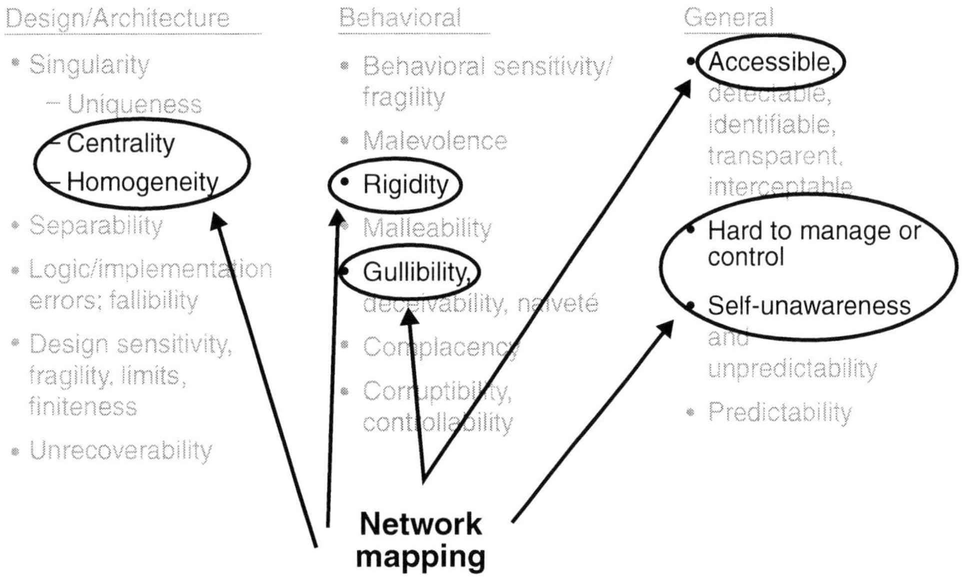

Figure 4.4—Vulnerabilities Enabling Network Mapping

Finally, consider Trojan horse attacks on a computer system. Figure 4.5 shows that Trojan horses exploit not only gullibility (the traditional concept from the story of the Trojan horse) but other vulnerabilities as well. A Trojan horse can enter a system when gullible software trusts too much of the data submitted to it, gullible users open email attachments that appear suspicious to the trained eye, or gullible users load software from uncertified sites. Homogeneity makes it easier to focus an attack on a single type of target and compromise systems across the organization. Controllability allows the Trojan to take over computers and use them for other exploits and attacks. Self-unawareness prevents the user from detecting not only the initial Trojan horse but also indicators that the computer has been compromised and is being controlled for other purposes. Difficulty in managing one's system implies that it may be hard to reassert control and delete the Trojan once it has infected the system. Finally, accessibility allows the Trojan horse to present itself to the system or user in the first place.

RANDMR1601-4.5

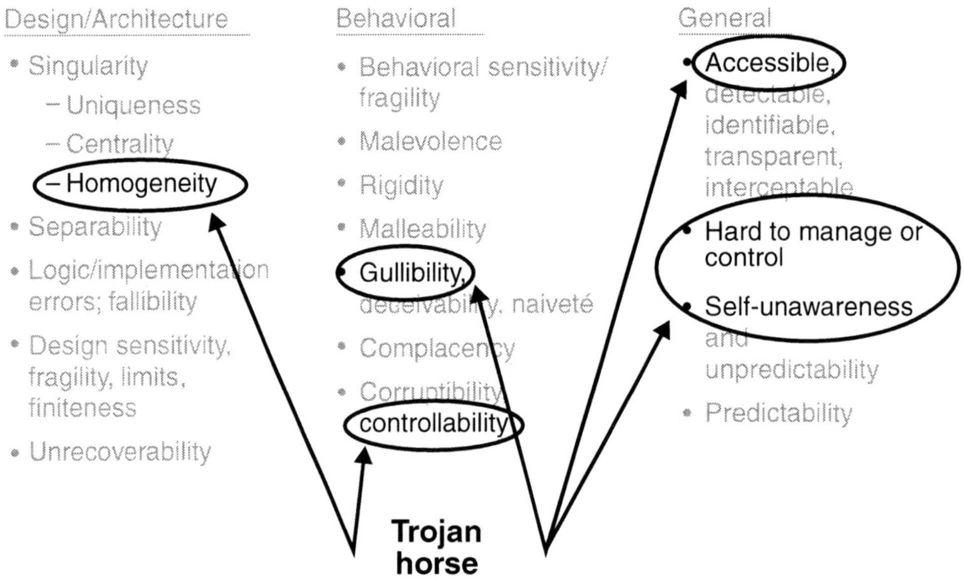

Figure 4.5—Vulnerabilities Enabling Trojan Horse Attacks

Chapter Five

DIRECT AND INDIRECT SECURITY TECHNIQUES

This chapter provides an in-depth description of information system security techniques that help to mitigate vulnerabilities. Techniques are grouped according to the fundamental concepts they employ. These security technique categories are what the matrix and filters in step 4 recommend based on the types of vulnerability attributes, user role, and attack/failure stage in question.

The chapter ends by describing how some well-known security approaches rely on one or more of these fundamental categories.

SECURITY TECHNIQUE CATEGORIES AND EXAMPLES

The security field has identified and developed a large number of security techniques, employing various strategies to mitigate vulnerabilities. Some techniques make system objects resilient to attacks or failures. Other techniques enable active identification and response to attacks or failures. Additional techniques block critical attack components or failure causes from reaching the object. Further techniques deter attackers from even trying an attack in the first place. Figure 5.1 lists the major techniques of relevance to information system objects, grouped by whether they improve the resilience or robustness of the object from attack or failure, whether they improve knowledge and awareness of an attack or failure, whether they deny knowledge and awareness to an attacker, or whether they deter and punish attackers. Many of these techniques overlap and complement each other, but the categories provide important distinctions and properties in and of themselves.

Resilience and Robustness

The first general category of security techniques involves making the system more resilient and robust to attack.

Heterogeneity. Heterogeneity includes component types, operating ranges, manufacturers, expertise, background, etc.; randomized compilation creating diversity; multimedia; and parallel heterogeneity (e.g., parallel email programs with synchronization).

RANDMR1601-5.1

Resilience/Robustness

- Heterogeneity
- Redundancy
- Centralization
- Decentralization
- VV&A; SW/HW engineering; evaluations; testing
- Control of exposure, access, and output
- Trust learning and enforcement systems
- Non-repudiation
- Hardening
- Fault, uncertainty, validity, and quality tolerance and graceful degradation
- Static resource allocation
- Dynamic resource allocation
- Management
- Threat response structures and plans
- Rapid reconstitution and recovery
- Adaptability and learning
- Immunological defense systems
- Vaccination

ISR and Self-Awareness

- Intelligence operations
- Self-awareness, monitoring, and assessments
- Deception for ISR
- Attack detection, recognition, damage assessment, and forensics (self and foe)

Counterintelligence, Denial of ISR and Target Acquisition

- General counterintelligence
- Deception for CI
- Denial of ISR and target acquisition

Deterrence and Punishment

- Deterrence
- Preventive and retributive information/military operations
- Criminal and legal penalties and guarantees
- Law enforcement; civil proceedings

Figure 5.1—Categories of Security Mitigation Techniques

Redundancy. Redundancy includes alternative systems and/or methods to accomplish what a system does. The evaluator should also consider path diversity, bi- or n-connectedness, mirroring of databases, excess capacity, and stockpiling.

Centralization. Centralization includes the following: central collection of information, reporting, alerting, repairs, and updates to gain a common operating picture of physical systems, quality control, cost savings, etc.; and centralized location of management (or virtual centralization via communications) to provide consistency, coordination, etc.

Decentralization. The evaluator should consider decentralized control points, routing, backups, configuration data, repair points, staff; distributed, mobile processing; rotated responsibilities; and redundant information at different places.

VV&A, Software and Hardware Engineering, Evaluations, or Testing. The broad area of rigorous design and engineering of information system components includes quality information system production; procedural certification (e.g., the Capability Maturity Model[1]); personnel and system testing, training, licensing, and certification; security procedures, checklists, and checks; security modeling, evaluation, and test-

[1] See www.sei.cmu.edu/cmm/.

ing; red teaming (e.g., general security, intrusions, clearances, access); and exercises (real, simulated, tabletop).

Control of Exposure, Access, and Output. Controlling the boundary of the information system is the most common area of attention in information security. Techniques include cryptography, encryption, and public key infrastructures (PKIs); passwords, synchronized pseudorandom number generators; biometrics; smart cards; firewalls, filters, behavior limits; guards (ingress and egress); one-way gateways; backdoor elimination; uncopyable media or information; self-protecting packaging; air-gapped and off-line systems and backups; classification and compartmentalization (insider access based on privileges, clearances, roles, capability, or behavior); data, code, and process segmentation; wrapping trusted components (protect); wrapping, quarantining, or segregating untrusted components (control behavior and contain any damage); I/O checking (error checking, tight type and range checking, etc.); physical security measures (e.g., electromagnetic shielding, fences, barriers, security guards, proper distance from barriers, locks, positive or negative air pressure, etc.); using meta-data in support of classification, identification, and reasoning functions; nondisclosure during transit (encryption); and integrity verification.

Trust Learning and Enforcement Systems. Trust should be the basis of permitting access, acting on data, and using system components from others (e.g., software and files). Specific approaches include recording lessons learned, using consensus techniques, administering trust and experience surveys, collecting shared experience, and using trusted third parties to validate information and components.

Non-Repudiation. Techniques that prevent repudiation (and its earlier stage of attribution) include proof of receipt and ownership; authentication; PKI; and recording all accesses, read/writes, and data sources (sign-in and sign-out logs, video monitor, access logs, meta-data structures, etc.).

Hardening. Hardening an object to withstand attacks that get through protections can be a final, yet important, stand. Approaches include hardened electronics; error-correcting codes and software; robust staff and procedures (even if only a subset of components remains to provide minimal capability); EMP, environmental, shock, or surge-tolerant equipment; read-only (write-protect) data storage, configurations, network tables, etc.; and read-only memory (ROM).

Fault, Uncertainty, Validity, and Quality Tolerance and Graceful Degradation. Similar to hardening, tolerance and graceful degradation allows the object to tolerate faults, uncertainty, invalidity, and poor quality by adjusting behavior and performance to accommodate the problems without failing. Techniques include separability (to allow isolation of faulty components); tolerance built into design and approach; minimal ways to operate degraded equipment (e.g., running the fans in an air conditioner when the cooling components fail; running central processing units [CPUs] in protected modes or from minimal operating systems on disks with minimal extensions, graphics, etc.); ability to handle and reason with uncertain, partially reliable, and degraded data; accreditation of incoming information to quantify its reliability or uncertainty; validity assessment; source verification; providing metadata for data quality; and uncertainty reasoning and semantics.

Static Resource Allocation. Allocating resources in predefined ways allows time for advanced planning, analyzing the consequences of changes, and looking at their implications for improving the system's security posture. Approaches include restricting nonessential connections; reducing load at weak points; and establishing and implementing guidelines related to known sensitivities of systems (e.g., in Windows systems, limiting the number of applications open at the same time; keeping the use of unstable applications down to a minimum, especially at more critical times in a mission).

Dynamic Resource Allocation. The adaptive partner to static resource allocation, dynamic resource allocation utilizes information about the threat or problem to adjust resources in or near real time, often involving complex and changing responses. Techniques include load shedding (demand, throughput, heat, power, etc.); prioritizing clients or processes (e.g., market-based, managed priorities); cutting off offending traffic or allocations farther upstream; dynamic administrative overhead levels; dynamic network reconfiguration that is either manual or automated, and rule-driven, case-based, or searched (e.g., genetic algorithms or exploratory modeling);[2] keeping the use of unstable hardware or software down to a minimum at more critical times in a mission; and dynamic changes to provide unpredictability or deception.

General Management. Effective management can improve security through reporting systems, structures, and procedures; quality control; ensuring that default settings meet security needs; peer pressure; information dissemination and advertising; training; security campaigns and reminders; warnings and threats; policy reminders and motivators; and red teaming to test and evaluate procedures and compliance.

Threat Response Structures and Plans. Information Conditions (INFOCONs) and other preplanned static and dynamic protective measures employ a hierarchy of increasing information system protective measures to be taken in response to anticipated or observed attack threat levels. Other approaches include data and configuration protection and backup; establishment of backup servers; infrastructure backup; security plans and MOUs; crisis planning and management; purging and filtering; adaptive response to adaptive attacks; and resource reallocation.

Rapid Reconstitution and Recovery. The ability to reconstitute or recover after a failure can be almost as effective as not having failed in the first place if the response time is rapid enough relative to the performance needs of the system. Techniques include data protection and recovery; warm rebooting; hot, warm, or cold backup servers; reserved and alternate channels to "reboot"; having reserve staff available

---

[2]For example, networks can be reconfigured to accommodate new loads, bypass unauthorized traffic, or facilitate priority traffic based on available network management information. New configurations can be constructed by employing heuristic rules, searching through prior cases, or searching over the space of simulated performance models (e.g., using exploratory modeling or genetic algorithms) to find a good reconfiguration for the current condition.

(either directly or through MOUs with nearby organizations); giving each network node a "genome" (predefined instruction set) for rebooting; infrastructure backup and recovery approaches; threat response plans (e.g., security plans, MOUs for prearranged coordination, or crisis planning and management); dynamic resource allocation (e.g., purging and filtering); adaptive response to adaptive attacks; manual operation and recovery plans; locally available replacement parts (possibly in different areas to provide a decentralized target); rapid replacement plans; local repair capabilities; and examining what hardware, software, and data are the hardest to regenerate (and thus need to be preserved or made redundant).

Adaptability and Learning. Adversaries continually learn about targets and adapt to changing defenses. A defender, therefore, must adapt to these changing threats or run the risk of being outpaced by a creative adversary that can simply bypass the defender's "Maginot Line."[3] Techniques include building adaptive responses to unknown or adaptive attacks; extracting lessons learned and creating best security practices databases (a gross "immunological system" from one perspective); leveraging centralization to improve dissemination of lessons learned about attacks; mining attack data to learn what the adversary is doing, develop protective actions, and develop countermeasures; ensuring sufficient monitoring and tracking to inform learning; developing available (rapid) training materials and critical data materials, especially on the critical operations and procedures for rapid use by secondary staff; and establishing dynamic INFOCONs and other threat response structures and plans.

Immunological Defense Systems. Borrowing from biology, an "immunological" system incorporates threat recognition, mitigation development, implementation, and dissemination across the system and organization. Techniques include automatic (preferred) or manual systems to detect threats, spread warnings, install updates or patches, and enact security measures; automatic commercial off-the-shelf (COTS) patch and profile data updates; memory, adaptation, and communication (requires a reporting structure); sharing information globally on attacks to piece together what is happening and how to respond; and applying concepts to develop adaptive and shared INFOCON procedures.

Vaccination. Another concept inspired by biology involves the deliberate attack ("infection") to train, recognize, sensitize, and prepare for future attacks (with or without a formal "immunological system"). Red teaming to sensitize the system is one such approach.

---

[3]The Maginot Line was a French network of defensive weapon emplacements and supporting tunnels designed to thwart potential physical attacks along the German boarder after World War I. The concept proved obsolete in World War II because of Germany's ability to rapidly end-run the line and attack from an unprotected angle.

Intelligence, Surveillance, Reconnaissance, and Self-Awareness

The second general category of security techniques involves collecting information about the threat and one's own system—in a sense, the "intelligence preparation of the battlefield."

Intelligence Operations. Intelligence involves the full range of information gathering about opponent (goals, thrusts, methods, capabilities, etc.) and insider operations. Ideally, intelligence covers both your and your opponent's information systems, since they constitute the "battlespace." Intelligence not only can detect attacks but can also gather advanced information that can inform protective and reactive procedures.

Self-Awareness, Monitoring, and Assessments. Knowing about your own system, being able to monitor it, and assessing its condition is often a critical step in recognizing and then mitigating attacks and failures. Techniques include self-monitoring (insider or outsider threats); security audits (e.g., the VAM methodology and IVA); red teaming to gather information; network monitoring and management tools; state and performance monitors; documentation of your system's configurations and states; static modeling and understanding; monitoring and recording the behavior of applications and staff (data accessed or changed; connections; requests; functions executed; accesses attempted; etc.); and providing capabilities for remote monitoring from centralized locations for expert consultations and monitoring.

Deception for ISR. Deception can be a useful (and unexpected) technique for intelligence, surveillance, and reconnaissance (ISR), since by its very nature deception affects information flow. Techniques include sting and intelligence operations using honeypots, cutouts, zombies, decoys, disguise, structural or behavioral mimicry, etc.[4]

Attack Detection, Recognition, Damage Assessment, and Forensics (Self and Foe). Various methods are available to detect, recognize, and analyze attacks, as well as assess the scope of the damage from these attacks. Techniques include real-time intrusion detection; learning systems (neural nets, self-organizing maps, etc.); pattern recognition (case-based, rule-based, model-based correlation, etc.); self-/non-self-discrimination; internal system behavior and condition monitoring; deception for detection and recognition (e.g., spoofing, canaries, honeypots); tamper and unsealing detection; tracking and tracing; special monitoring privileges; corruption recognition; use of design specifications to bound acceptable hardware, software, and staff behavior; tamper-evident barriers; non-repudiation mechanisms (e.g., modification records, proofs of receipt and ownership, authentication, PKI); access logs; and global sharing of intelligence data to aid in analysis.

---

[4]See Gerwehr and Glenn (2000, Chapter 3) for a review of general deception techniques.

Counterintelligence; Denial of ISR and Target Acquisition

The third general category of security techniques involves CI, as well as denying ISR and target acquisition to your adversary—directly affecting your adversary's ability to gather required knowledge about your system for an attack.

General CI. Some basic CI techniques for information systems include scans for physical monitors, bugs, etc.; scans for software Trojan horses and monitors; security checks; and polygraphs.

Unpredictable to Adversary. Making your system unpredictable prevents the adversary from making educated guesses about your system based on industry standard configurations and components. Techniques include pseudorandomization and uncommon configurations, names, locations, equipment, responsibilities, etc.; extreme heterogeneity or decentralization; removing documentation; self-organizing collective behavior; goal-oriented behavior; specialization; adaptive, threat-based, or rule-based activity; communication among individuals; beneficial emergent behavior unpredictable by outsiders (or even insiders); and varied operating procedures (hardware, software, staff).

Deception for CI. As with ISR, deception can be a useful (and unexpected) technique for CI by interrupting information flow to the adversary. Deception techniques for CI include masking an item and its particular vulnerabilities; masking real and putting out false architecture, design, and plan information; and misleading or confusing the adversary. *Masking* involves camouflage; low observables; mislabeling; removing labels; producing false associated plans, procedures, instructions, data, or other information; network anonymizers (anonymous searches, IP spoofing, etc.); emission shielding; power controls; and behavioral camouflage or mimicry (acting more like something that is not a target). *Misleading* involves stings; cutouts and zombies; decoys; disguises, mimicry (looking more like something that is not a target but is also not noise); honeypots; disinformation (e.g., locations, capabilities, configurations, procedures, vulnerabilities, etc.); bluffs and feints; and disinformation. *Confusing* involves oversaturation; paralyzing uncertainty; "shoot-and-scoot"; making an attack seem easier than it really is; producing a false sense of security in the adversary; and disinformation.

Denial of ISR and Target Acquisition. Direct denial techniques include movement, shielding or access filters, and jamming.

Deterrence and Punishment

The last general category of security techniques involves intimidating adversaries to reduce their willingness to attack your system in the first place.

Deterrence. Various deterrence techniques for information systems include credible threats; shows of force; warnings, peer pressure, psychological operations (PsyOps), and tamper-evident and damage-evident devices (e.g., tape, tabs, indicators); and proper management of the implementation of deterrence.

Preventive and Retributive Information/Military Operations. Offensive IO[5] and military operations can be used as preventive and retributive responses to attacks from adversaries. Operation aspects include information dissemination, PsyOps, electronics warfare, physical attack, and information attack.

Criminal and Legal Penalties and Guarantees. Techniques that can be employed include bonding; guarantees; warrantees; international treaties and agreements; utilize non-repudiation data; and penalties for attacks and damage (including by insiders).

Law Enforcement; Civil Proceedings. Finally, enforcement of laws is important; otherwise their threats will be hollow. Enforcement aspects include international, national, state, and local authorities and courts; utilizing non-repudiation data; and proper follow-through and management.

HOW SECURITY TECHNIQUES COMBINE IN COMMON SECURITY APPROACHES

The following examples demonstrate how the fundamental mitigation techniques listed above are combined in common security approaches.

First, consider INFOCONs. Figure 5.2 shows that the INFOCON concept is an objective threat response (or preparation) plan that allows advanced analysis and arrangements. However, effective use of INFOCONs also relies on the ability to monitor and assess one's own system to understand what the threat really is and to ensure that the INFOCON level is neither too low nor too high given the real threat. The monitoring and assessment aspect is important to prevent the known concern that the INFOCON level may be set too high, incurring reduced system performance due to heightened security.

Second, consider "Indications and Warning" (I&W) systems that provide intelligence on attacks. Figure 5.3 shows that I&W relies on a whole host of ISR and self-awareness techniques. The current state of I&W for IO relies mostly on monitoring and detection techniques within the defender's systems (e.g., intrusion-detection systems, network monitors, deception techniques) rather than on intelligence operations in the general Internet or in an adversary's organizations and computer systems.

Third, consider Computer Emergency Response Teams (CERTs) and other related centers that coordinate computer security, conduct vulnerability and threat analyses, provide advisories, organize and plan security responses, and implement responses (both planned and ad hoc) during attacks.[6] Figure 5.4 shows that CERTs employ

---

[5]Information operations can also be referred to as information warfare (IW).

[6]Example CERTs include the "CERT® Coordination Center" (CERT®CC) (www.cert.org), DoD-CERT (www.cert.mil), Army Computer Emergency Response Team (ACERT), and AIR FORCE Computer Emergency Response Team (AFCERT). Related centers include the Federal Computer Incident Response Center (FedCIRC) (www.fedcirc.gov), the National Infrastructure Protection Center (NIPC) (www.nipc.gov), Naval

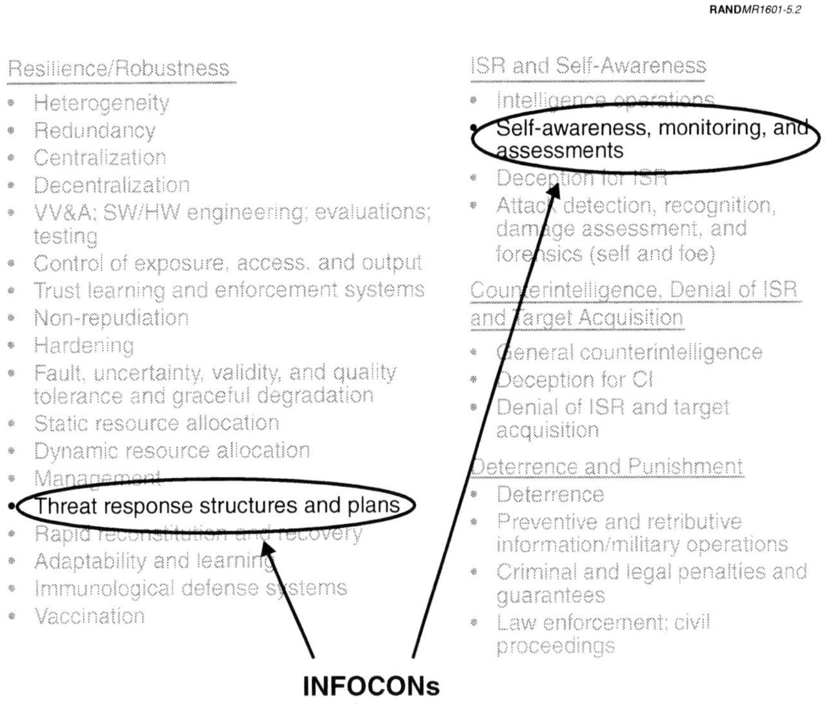

Figure 5.2—Security Techniques Supporting INFOCONs

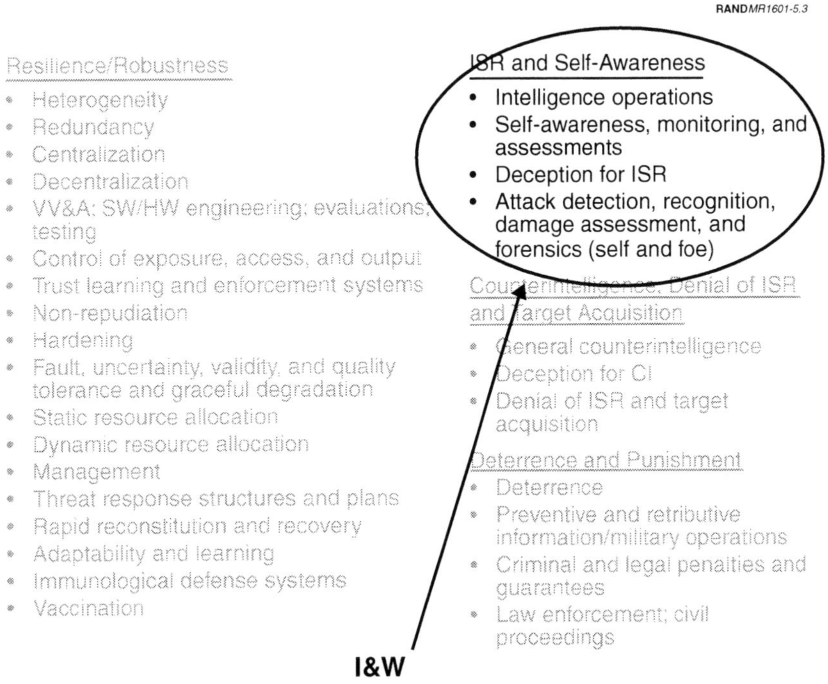

Figure 5.3—Security Techniques Supporting I&W

Computer Incident Response Team (NAVCIRT), and the NASA Incident Response Center (NASIRC) (www-nasirc.nasa.gov).

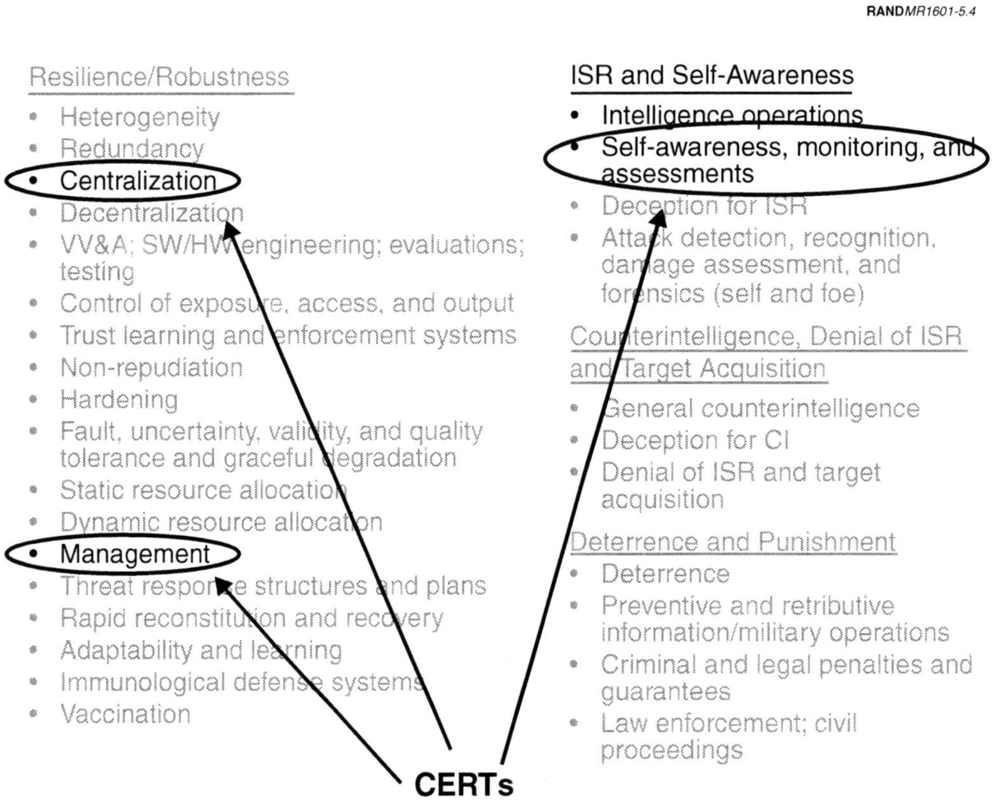

Figure 5.4—Security Techniques Supporting CERTs

centralization to coordinate monitoring, security procedures and other information, security responses, management, and communications against attacks.

Fourth, consider firewalls that filter information and requests for service coming into a local network based on predefined (and sometimes adaptive) profiles. Figure 5.5 shows that firewalls directly implement a primary means of controlling exposure, access, and information output, but effective firewall maintenance depends on current intelligence, assessments of threats, and knowledge of what is happening within one's system.

Fifth, consider encryption and PKIs. Figure 5.6 shows that they provide a critical technical means for controlling exposure, access, and output by verifying identity and controlling exposure of information during transit.

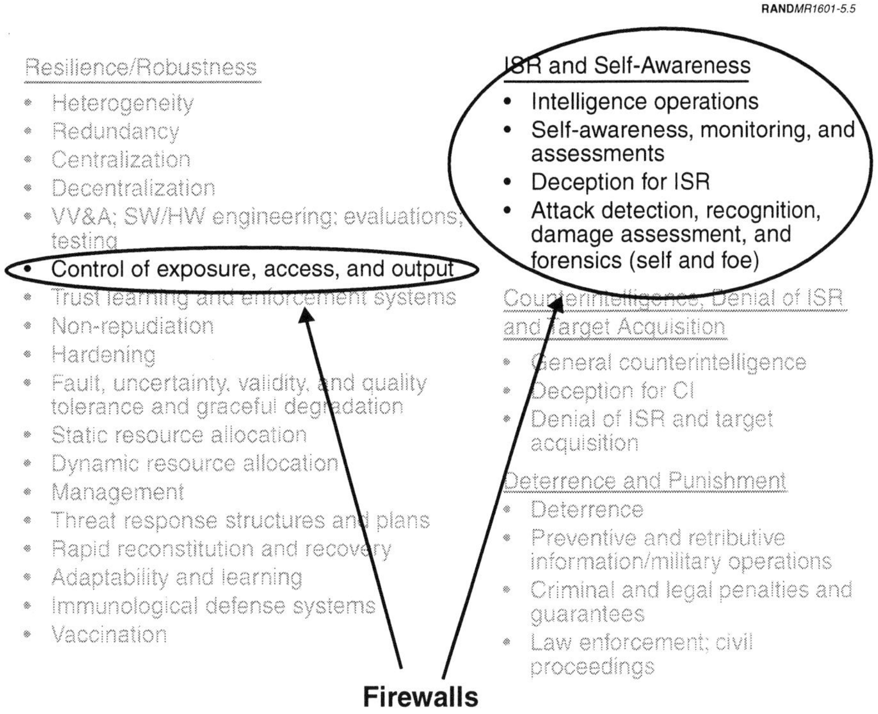

Figure 5.5—Security Techniques Used in Firewalls

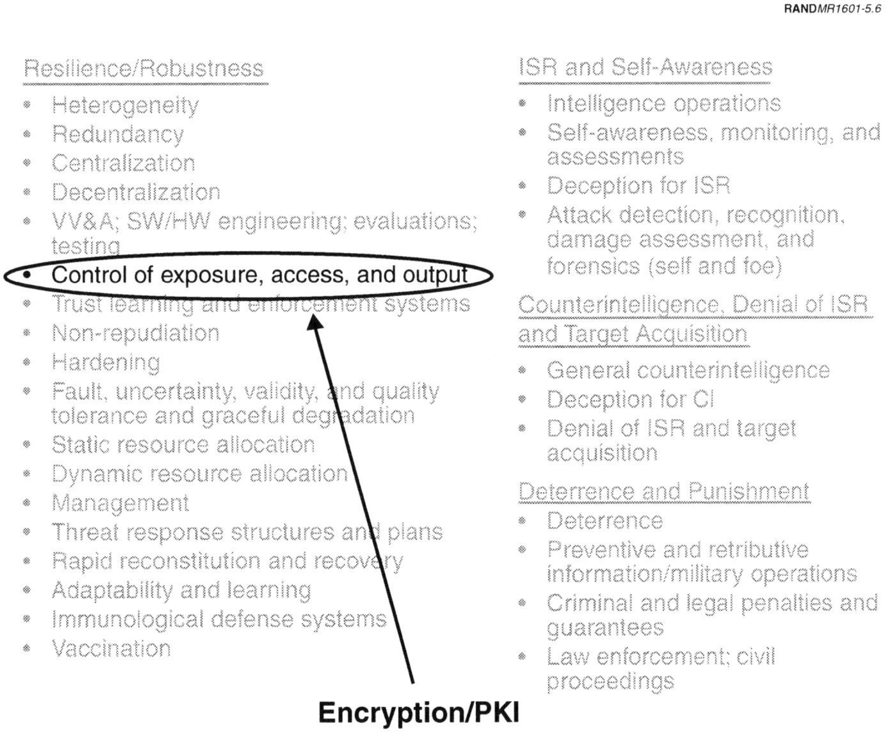

Figure 5.6—Security Technique Incorporating Encryption and PKIs

Finally, consider isolation and air-gapped networks. Figure 5.7 shows that isolation and air gapping are other technical means for controlling exposure, access, and output. The most critical information systems often use these approaches, since electronic filters, firewalls, and encryption schemes can be compromised with enough effort. Air gapping raises the level of security so that other access means have to be developed by the adversary (e.g., developing physical access, using insiders, or so-called "chipping" in which physical devices are inserted or modified to facilitate future access or damage).

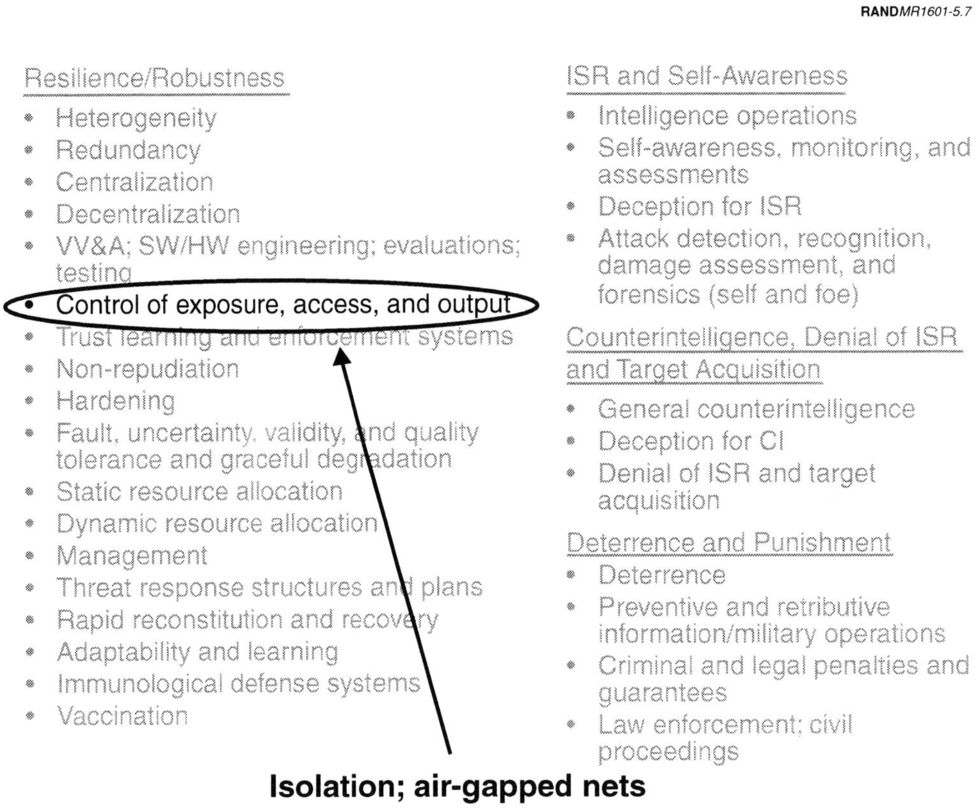

Figure 5.7—Security Technique Incorporating Isolation of Systems

Chapter Six

GENERATING SECURITY OPTIONS FOR VULNERABILITIES

This chapter describes how step 4 of the VAM methodology maps the vulnerabilities presented in Chapter Four to the security techniques presented in Chapter Five to provide specific guidance on how to address identified vulnerabilities. Next, the chapter describes filtering techniques that improve the appropriateness of the security techniques identified in the matrix to a particular user type and attack stage. Chapters Five and Six describe step 4 of the methodology and support the selection of security techniques (step 5). Finally, the chapter provides specific examples of the kinds of specific security countermeasures that can be identified for specific, common information system vulnerabilities by an operational evaluator employing the methodology.

MAPPING VULNERABILITIES TO SECURITY TECHNIQUES

Once the often-challenging task of identifying both known and unknown vulnerabilities has been achieved, the evaluator must identify which of the many security techniques identified in Chapter Five are relevant to the vulnerabilities from Chapter Four identified during the evaluation. Rather than leaving this task to unguided personal intuition or blind brainstorming, the VAM methodology guides the evaluator by explicitly identifying in a matrix which security techniques are relevant for each vulnerability attribute.

Security Techniques That Address Vulnerabilities

Table 6.1 shows the large matrix in the methodology that relates vulnerability properties (see Chapter Four) along the left column to the security techniques (see Chapter Five) across the top row. The kinds of relationships between individual vulnerability properties and security techniques are represented by numeric values (see Figure 6.1). These numeric values were determined by experience and judgment about the logical relationships between broad categories of vulnerabilities and techniques. The reasoning behind each value is documented in the Appendix.

Table 6.1
The Vulnerability to Security Technique Matrix

RANDMR1601-table6.1

Attributes Leading to Vulnerabilities		Resilience / Robustness	Resilience/Robustness																		ISR and Self-Awareness				CI, Denial of ISR & Target Acquisition				Deterrence and Punishment			
								Trust, Authentication, and Access							Management																	
		Resilience / Robustness	Heterogeneity	Redundancy	Centralization	Decentralization	VV&A, SW/HW Engineering, Evaluations, Testing	Control of Exposure, Access, and Output	Trust Learning and Enforcement Systems	Non-Repudiation	Hardening	Fault, Uncertainty, Validity, and Quality Tolerance and Graceful Degradation	Static Resource Allocation	Dynamic Resource Allocation	General Management	Threat Response Structures and Plans	Rapid Reconstitution and Recovery	Adaptability and Learning	Immunological Defense Systems	Vaccination	Intelligence Operations	Self-Awareness, Monitoring, and Assessments	Deception for ISR	Attack Detection, Recognition, Damage Assessment, and Forensics (Self and Foe)	General Counter-Intelligence	Unpredictable to Adversary	Deception for CI	Denial of ISR & Target Acquisition	Deterrence	Preventive and Retributive Information/Military Operations	Criminal and Legal Penalties and Guarantees	Law Enforcement; Civil Proceedings
Design/Architecture	Singularity	2	2	2	1 −1	2	2	2	1	1	2	2	1	1	1	2	2	2			1	1			1	1	1	1				
	Uniqueness	2	2	2	1	1	2	2			2	2	1	1	1 −1	2	2				1	1			1	1	1	1			1	
	Centrality	2	1	1	0 −2	2	2	2 −1	1	1	2	2	−1	−1	1 −2	2 −1	1	0	1 −1		1 −1	1 −1	0 −1	−1	1	1	1	1		2		0
	Homogeneity	2	2	1	−1	1	2	1			2	2	0	0	1 −2	−1	0		0 −1	0 −1		1			1	1	1	1				
	Separability	2		−1	2	−2	2	1 −2	1 −1		1	2	−2	−1	2	−2		1	1	1	1 −1	2	0	−1	1 −1	1 −1	1 −1	1				
	Logic/ Implementation Errors; Fallibility	2	2		1	1 −1	2	2	1		2	2	1	1	2	1 −1	1	2	2	2		1			1	1	1	1			1	1
	Design Sensitivity/ Fragility/Limits/ Finiteness	2	2 −1	2	1	2 −1	2	2 −1			2 −1	2 −1	2	2	2 −1	1 −1	1	1	1	1	1	2	0	1	1	1	1	1			1	1
	Unrecoverability	2	2	2	1	2	2	1 −1			2	2	1	1	1	1	2	1	1	1	1	2		1	1	1	1	1			1	1
Behavior	Behavioral Sensitivity/Fragility	2	2 −1	2 −1	1	2 −1	2	2 −1			2	2	2	2 −1	2	1 −1	1	1 −1	1	1	1	2		1	1 −1	1 −1	1 −1	1			1	1
	Malevolence		1	1		1	2	2	2	2					2	1			1	1 −1	2	2	2	2	2	2	2	2	2	2	2	2
	Rigidity	2	1		−2	1	2	−2	2		−2	2	1 −2	2	2 −1	2 −2	2	2	2	2		1		1	1	1	1	1	−1			
	Malleability		1		1	1 −1	2	1	2 −1	1	2		1 −1	−1	2	2		1 −1	−1			2		1	1	1	1	1	2		1	
	Gullibility/ Deceivability/ Naiveté					−1	2	1 −1	2 −1	1	2		1 −2	−1	2 −1	2 −2		2 −1	1	2	2	2		1	1 −1	1 −1	1	1				
	Complacency	2			1 −1		2 −1	1 −1	2 −1	−1	−1	−1	−1	2 −1	2 −1	2 −1	−1	2	2 −1	1	2 −1	2 −1		1	1	1	1		2 −1		1 −1	−1
	Corruptibility/ Controllability	2	1		1 −1	1	2	2 −1	2	1	2			−1	2				2 −1	1 −1	2	2		1	1	1	1		2		1	
General	Accessible/ Detectable/ Identifiable/ Transparent/ Interceptable	2	1	1	−2	2	2	2	2		2	2			1	2 −1			1	1	1	1 −1		1	2	2	2	2	2	2	1	1
	Hard to Manage or Control		−2	−1	2	−2	2	2 −1	2		−1		2	2 −1	2	2		−1	1			2	−1	1	−1	−1	−1		1		1	1
	Self Unawareness and Unpredictability		−2		2	−2	2	−1	2		−1	−1	1	1 −1	1	1 −1		−1	2	2		2	−1	2	1	1 −2	1 −2					
	Predictability		2		−1	1	2 −1	1 −1			−1		−2	2 −1	1 −1	1 −1		2	2 −1	1 −1			0	1	2	2	2	2	−1			

NOTE: The key for this table is in Figure 6.1.

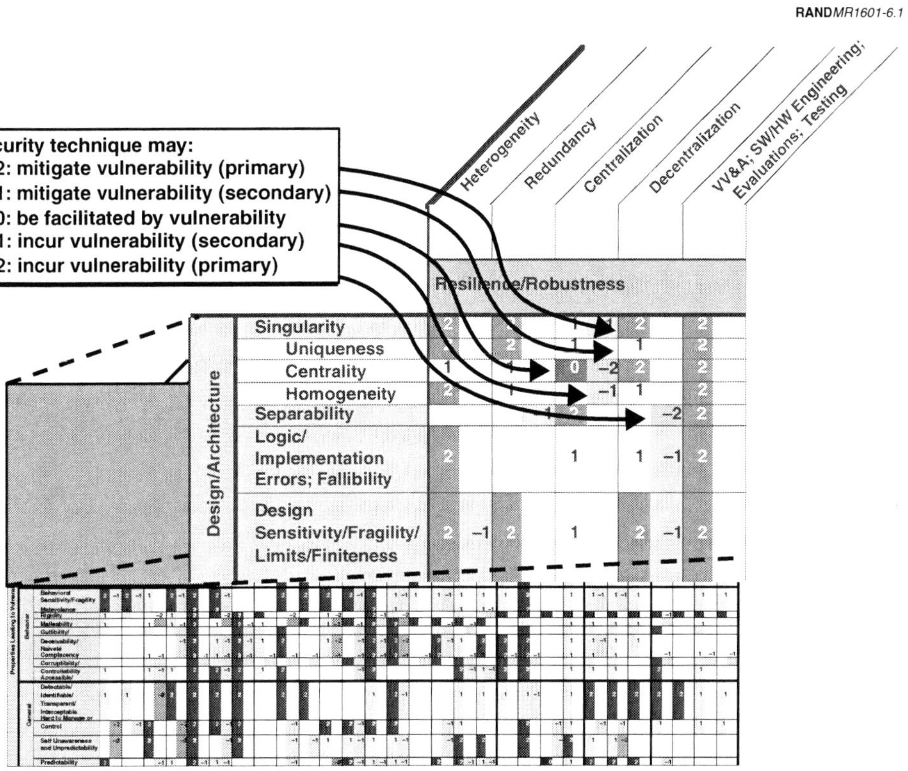

Figure 6.1—Values Relating Vulnerabilities to Security Techniques

When a security technique has the potential to mitigate a vulnerability, the matrix contains a numeral *2* or *1* at the intersection point. A *2* indicates that the security technique is a *primary mitigation* candidate, and a *1* indicates that the technique is a *secondary mitigation* candidate (recall Figure 3.4). Therefore, when one identifies a vulnerability, he or she can look across the row and see what security techniques could be of primary and secondary relevance to that vulnerability by looking for techniques that have a *2* or *1* (respectively) in its column for the vulnerability row.

For example, in the enlargement in Figure 6.1, an evaluator with a *Singularity* vulnerability should first consider *Heterogeneity*; *Redundancy*; *Decentralization*; and *VV&A, SW/HW Engineering, Evaluations, Testing* to help mitigate the singularity.[1] *Centralization* may be considered as a secondary candidate once the evaluator considers all the primary candidates.

Security Techniques That Incur Vulnerabilities

Interestingly, security techniques can also incur new vulnerabilities when they are implemented. These cases are noted in the matrix using negative numerals *–2* and *–1*

[1]Other techniques are also rated as primary using a *2* but are not visible in the enlargement.

at the intersection point. A *–2* indicates a *primary caution* where the security technique often incurs the vulnerability, and a *–1* indicates a *secondary caution*. Therefore, when one considers any security technique, he or she should look down the entire column for that technique and see what vulnerability cautions can be of primary and secondary relevance to that technique. This identification can be of use regardless of the driving factor for the security technique and can help evaluators audit existing security programs in searching for hidden vulnerabilities.

For example, in the enlargement in Figure 6.1, an evaluator considering the implementation of a *Centralization* effort (or looking for vulnerabilities that may be present due to existing centralizations) is given (among other things) a primary caution (*–2*) that *Centrality* problems may be introduced.[2] The evaluator is also given a secondary caution (*–1*) that *Homogeneity* may be introduced, since centralization efforts often involve standardization of equipment, software, human/social structures, and infrastructure reliance.

Vulnerability Properties Can Sometimes Facilitate Security Techniques

Finally, in constructing the matrix we noticed instances in which a "vulnerability" might have beneficial side effects that facilitate security techniques. These instances are noted with the numeral *0* at the intersection point between the vulnerability property and security technique.

An obvious example is the fact that *Centrality* facilitates *Centralization,* since the concept can be viewed both as a potential vulnerability and a technique for addressing problems. A less obvious example is when *Homogeneity* can facilitate both *Static* and *Dynamic Resource Allocation* by providing a uniform set of system components that are more easily interchanged and granted responsibilities. *Homogeneity* can also facilitate *Rapid Recovery and Reconstitution* since interchangeable parts, common spares, and reduced logistics allow faster recovery. In a final example, *Predictability* can be exploited by *Deception for ISR* techniques to observe how an adversary reacts to predictable situations, yielding clues to their tool set and sophistication.

The matrix does not identify facilitative relationships between security techniques, but they do exist. Recall the examples in Chapter Five of security concepts (e.g., INFOCONs, I&W, CERTs, firewalls) that rely on the combined effect from different security techniques (see Figures 5.2, 5.3, 5.4, and 5.5, respectively).

Striking a Balance

The interplay between security techniques that mitigate vulnerabilities and security techniques that incur vulnerabilities demonstrates the competing nature of concerns in the security world. Too much of a good thing can be damaging in the security world as well. There are usually balances that must be struck

[2]Centrality can be both a vulnerability and a positive security technique.

- when weighing the investments in system functionality versus security
- among degrees of implementation of a security technique
- between competing goals and characteristics in security
- among the added costs of implementing a security approach to minimize or prevent adding vulnerabilities and the security benefits from the implementation.

For example, in the enlargement in Figure 6.1, an evaluator trying to deal with a *Singularity* should consider *Decentralization* (among other things), but decentralization may introduce *Separability* problems (primary concerns), as well as *Logic/ Implementation Errors* and *Design Sensitivity/Fragility* problems (secondary concerns). The evaluator needs to weigh the singularity risks against the costs and risks of decentralization implementation options. Can decentralization be implemented to address the particular type of singularity? Can decentralization be implemented in such a way to minimize or prevent logic or implementation errors and design sensitivities or fragilities? In many cases, the awareness of these cautions can inform their design and implementation of the specific mitigation approaches taken, but they should be explicitly considered to balance the overall risk posture of the information system.

Design and Usage Considerations

These relationships do not specify the type of system objects possessing the vulnerabilities, specifics about the object implementation, and the general security posture in the system. Therefore, detailed information about the system under study and the appropriateness of security options must supplement the general knowledge reflected in the matrix. As a result, the matrix forms a *guide* to aid the evaluator through the huge space of options rather than a predefined prescription. In specific situations, vulnerabilities may also benefit from the use of security techniques unvalued in the matrix, so at times one may want to reach beyond the techniques called out in the matrix. New categories arising from security research will need to be added to the matrix over time.

REFINING THE SECURITY SUGGESTIONS

For each vulnerability property, the methodology matrix displayed in Table 6.1 identifies a rather large number of primary and secondary security techniques of potential relevance to consider. As the number of vulnerabilities increases, an almost unmanageable set of suggestions is generated. Although the VAM matrix is an improvement over methodologies that do not generate suggestions that help the evaluator reason through the security problem, additional help is needed to refine the selection process. Also, many of the security suggestions may be generally appropriate but beyond the purview and authority of the specific evaluator using the methodology, complicating the usability of the raw matrix. Therefore, to focus the evaluator's attention on the most relevant security techniques, the following filtering approaches have been developed based on the job role of the evaluator conducting a security assessment and the distinction of supporting stages in an information system attack as separate from the core attack (or failure) vulnerability.

Evaluator Job Roles

The first technique for filtering security suggestions utilizes the fact that there are different job roles an evaluator plays; security suggestions can be filtered or eliminated if they are not usable by the evaluator because of his or her responsibilities and authority. The methodology currently employs three evaluator job role categories: operational, development, and policy. *Operational* evaluators include system users, administrators, and managers who are either responsible for security or have concerns about the security of the systems they use. *Development* evaluators include research, development, testing, and system engineers responsible for creating and configuring the information system but are not engaged in its operational use. *Policy* evaluators specify the overall system needs, requirements, and operating procedures—often in the context of the larger use of the information systems. The list of evaluator types could be expanded or customized in the future, but these three types have been useful to date.

The first three rating columns in Table 6.2 and Table 6.3 identify which security techniques are strongly or weakly relevant to these three evaluator job roles. Strongly relevant security techniques are rated a *2* while weakly relevant security techniques are rated a *1*. For example, Table 6.2 shows that *Non-Repudiation, Management,* and *Threat Response Structures and Plans* are strongly relevant (rated *2*) to *Operational* evaluators (first rating column), since operational individuals and organizations can monitor users and access, establish and enforce management tools to improve security, and establish procedures and agreements to respond to threats and failures. *Control of Exposure, Access, and Output* is less relevant (rated *1*) because operational individuals and organizations can implement and control physical or cyber access but can be constrained in the design and implementation of software and procedures by the designs or policies implemented by others. So, for example, an operational user for which the main matrix (Table 6.1) suggests that three possible techniques—(i) *Heterogeneity,* (ii) *Non-Repudiation,* and (iii) *Control of Exposure, Access, and Output*—may help to mitigate a vulnerability of concern would first consider *Non-repudiation,* since it rates as strongly relevant (2) in Table 6.2. *Control of Exposure, Access, and Output* would be considered second since it rates as weakly relevant (1) in Table 6.2. The third matrix suggestion (*Heterogeneity*) would be considered last because it has no rating in Table 6.2.

It appears that developers have the most flexibility in security choices (i.e., have the most *2*s in their rating columns), since they design the architecture, physical plant, and infrastructure dependencies and relationships within the constrains of policies that are usually quite broad. However, developers cannot dictate to operational users exactly how they will use and manage their information systems. Thus, each job type has its own realm of responsibility, authority, and thus flexibility.

Table 6.2

Resilience and Robustness Techniques for Evaluator Job Roles and Attack Components

RANDMR1601-table6.2

2 Strongly relevant
1 Weakly relevant

	Apply to Physical, Cyber, Human/Social, and Infrastructure Components	Useful to These Users:			Helps Protect These Attack Stages				
		Operational	Developer	Policy	Knowledge	Access	Target	Non-Retribution	Assess
Resilience/Robustness	Heterogeneity		2	1	1	1	2		1
Resilience/Robustness	Redundancy		2	1			2		
Resilience/Robustness	Centralization		2		1	1	1		1
Resilience/Robustness	Decentralization		2		1	1	1		1
Resilience/Robustness	VV&A, SW/HW Engineering, Evaluations, Testing		2				2		
Trust, Authentication, and Access	Control of Exposure, Access, and Output	1	2		2	2	2		2
Trust, Authentication, and Access	Trust Learning and Enforcement Systems	1	2		1	2	2		1
Trust, Authentication, and Access	Non-Repudiation	2	2		1	2	2	2	1
Resilience/Robustness	Hardening		2				2		
Resilience/Robustness	Fault, Uncertainty, Validity, and Quality Tolerance and Graceful Degradation		2				2		
Resilience/Robustness	Static Resource Allocation	1	2				2		
Resilience/Robustness	Dynamic Resource Allocation		2		1		2		1
Management	General Management	2	2	2	1	2	2		1
Management	Threat Response Structures and Plans	2	2		1	2	2		1
Resilience/Robustness	Rapid Reconstitution and Recovery	1	2				2		
Resilience/Robustness	Adaptability and Learning	1	2		2		2		2

Table 6.3

ISR, CI, and Deterrence Techniques for Evaluator Job Roles and Attack Components

RANDMR1601-table6.3

2 Strongly relevant
1 Weakly relevant

	Apply to Physical, Cyber, Human/Social, and Infrastructure Components	Useful to These Users:			Helps Protect These Attack Stages				
		Operational	Developer	Policy	Knowledge	Access	Target	Non-Retribution	Assess
Intel, Surveillance, & Reconnaissance (ISR) and Self-Awareness	Intelligence Operations	2				1	1	1	
	Self-Awareness, Monitoring, and Assessments	2	2			1	1	1	
	Deception for ISR	2	2			1	1	1	
	Attack Detection, Recognition, Damage Assessment, and Forensics (Self and Foe)	2	2			1	1	1	
Counter-Intelligence / Denial of ISR & Target Acquisition	General Counter-Intelligence	2	2		2			2	2
	Unpredictable to Adversary	2	2		2			2	2
	Deception for CI	2	2		2			2	2
	Denial of ISR & Target Acquisition	2	2		2		1		
Offense and Retribution	Deterrence	2	2	2				2	
	Preventive and Retributive Information / Military Operations	2		2				2	
	Criminal and Legal Penalties and Guarantees		2	2				2	
	Law Enforcement; Civil Proceedings		2	2				2	

Attack Components

The second technique for filtering security suggestions utilizes the fact that while a failure may have a single vulnerability source, an attack on a system involves distinct components where security techniques can be employed. *Knowledge, access,* and *target vulnerabilities* are required in any successful attack. Complete prevention of any one of these three components will deny a successful attack, and protections across these components minimize the overall risk. Two other important attack components—*non-retribution* and the ability to *assess* the success of an attack—

while not critical to the success of an attack are so important to many attackers that an attack can be prevented if these components are denied.

Knowledge includes acquiring and understanding information about the target system, including general configuration information, security postures and procedures of the defender, ways to achieve access to the system, knowledge about the target vulnerability to be exploited, knowledge about the defender's indications and warning systems, procedures the defender uses to identify the attacker, and information to support attack assessments.

Access to the attacking system is required to acquire knowledge, perform the actual attack on the target, and assess the success of the attack. Access could be gained through each type of object (physical, cyber, human/social, and infrastructure) and include physical access or proximity (e.g., access to restricted areas or electromagnetic access); computer, communication, or control networks; agents with inside access; and vital infrastructure systems.

The **target vulnerability** or vulnerabilities to be exploited in the attack result from design weaknesses and behavioral sensitivities that can be exploited by an attacker. For vulnerabilities arising from natural or accidental causes, the target vulnerability category is the sole level of concern.

Non-retribution, while not critical to the success of every attack, is often very important to such attackers as nation-states that do not want their information attacks known, as well as organizations that worry about reprisals due to their own vulnerabilities.

Finally, complex organizations that rely on information attacks as components in larger operations need the ability to **assess** the effectiveness of their attacks (e.g., when other operations cannot proceed without knowing the success of the attack).

Table 6.4 lists the major ways that an attacker can accomplish each component of an attack (except the target vulnerability itself which is often a property of the information system itself and not under the purview of the attacker). These methods are distributed across the four major system objects (physical, cyber, human/social, and infrastructure). Table 6.5 identifies which vulnerability properties can be exploited in each of the five attack components.

Attack Stage Relevance by Evaluator Job Role

Taken together, evaluator role and attack stage filtering yields the following emergent effect that helps refine security suggestions. These filters focus attention on attack components in which the evaluator has more ability to implement protections and countermeasures. Thus, operational users generally have greater control over, knowledge of, and access to the systems than over their architecture and implementations. Developers can adjust the hardware and software to minimize vulnerabilities in the architecture and implementations but have less influence over use, knowledge, and access. Finally, policymakers set general guidance and constraints in design and operation but do not specify actual implementation details.

Table 6.4

Methods for Accomplishing Each Component of an Attack

RANDMR1601-table6.4

	Object of Vulnerability			
	Physical	**Cyber**	**Human/Social**	**Enabling Infrastructure**
Attack Stage	Hardware (Data Storage, Input/Output, Clients, Servers), Network and Communications, Locality	Software, Data, Information, Knowledge	Staff, Command, Management, Policies, Procedures, Training, Authentication	Ship, Building, Power, Water, Air, Environment
Knowledge	Viewable, blueprints, standard architecture, purchase orders, deductable from behavior or first principles (e.g., physics); hacker bulletin boards; chat rooms	Nmap port scan, open source information (e.g., Web); source code; reverse engineering; virus/worm reports; hacker bulletin boards; chat rooms; behavior of the system; blue prints; standard architectures; sniffers	Org. charts; "social engineering"; HUMINT	Viewable, blueprints, standard architecture, purchase orders, deductable from behavior or first principles (e.g., physics); hacker bulletin boards; chat rooms; Nmap port scan, open source information (e.g., Web); source code; reverse engineering; virus/worm reports; hacker bulletin boards; chat rooms; behavior of the system; blue prints; standard architectures; sniffers; Org. charts; "social engineering"; HUMINT
Access	Insider; visitors; neighborhood	Networks; EW	Phone; email; physical presence; agents; signals	Insider; visitors; neighborhood; networks; EW; phone; email; physical presence; agents; signals
Non-Retribution	Agents; disguises; camouflage	Spoofing; zombies	Agents; voice/communication disguises; camouflage	Agents; disguises; camouflage; spoofing; zombies; agents; voice/communication disguises; camouflage
Assess	Viewable, deductable from behavior or first principles (e.g., physics); insider; visitors; neighborhood	Nmap port scan, open source information (e.g., Web); news; virus/worm reports; hacker bulletin boards; chat rooms; behavior of the system; sniffers; networks	"Social engineering"; HUMINT; phone; email; physical presence; agents; signals	Viewable, deductable from behavior or first principles (e.g., physics); insider; visitors; neighborhood; Nmap port scan, open source information (e.g., Web); news; virus/worm reports; hacker bulletin boards; chat rooms; behavior of the system; sniffers; networks; "social engineering"; HUMINT; phone; email; physical presence; agents; signals

EXAMPLE SECURITY OPTIONS ARISING FROM THE USE OF THE METHODOLOGY

The following shows the kind of security options that an evaluator from an operational organization can generate, using the methodology as an analytical guide to addressing security concerns. These examples involve the common security concerns presented in Chapter Four in the checklist matrix example (see Table 4.3). These concerns range across cyber, physical, and human/social object of information systems for a number of different vulnerability attributes. The analysis in the examples is far from comprehensive, but it illustrates the use of the VAM methodology on well-known problems in the information security field and the types of specific security strategies that may come out of the analysis. Some security ideas are commonly known, while others are novel.

These generic examples do not contain specifics related to an actual vulnerability or more-specific examples of security techniques that address the vulnerabilities' unique characteristics. Nevertheless, they help to demonstrate how the methodology guides the evaluator to security techniques, and the kind of instantiations of the techniques that may be considered.

For each example, we specify the vulnerability attribute and object type followed by a short description of the vulnerability. We then highlight a number of security technique categories suggested by the matrix, along with specific mitigation strategies within the categories that may be appropriate for the particular vulnerability in question. These specific mitigation strategies arise both from the general list of security technique examples described in Chapter Five and from the novel countermeasures that came to us when we considered the security technique category afresh.

Insider Threat

Vulnerability Attribute: Malevolence.

Type of Target: Human/social.

It is widely believed that the "insider threat" (malevolent behavior by a trusted person with approved access to a critical information system) is the greatest threat to the security of information systems. The "insider" might be someone with a grudge, or someone co-opted by an enemy through blackmail, bribes, or the like.

Potential Relevant Mitigation Strategies:

Control of exposure, access, and output. Ensure that "insiders" have only that access within the network and physical areas needed for their jobs.

Non-repudiation. Maintain access and permissions audit logs to allow prosecution of anyone violating authorized procedures.

Table 6.5

Vulnerability Exploitation by Attack Component

RANDMR1601-table6.5

2 Strongly relevant
1 Weakly relevant

	Attributes	Used by Attacker for: Knowledge	Access	Target	Non-Retribution	Assess
Design/Architecture	Singularity			2		
	Uniqueness			2		
	Centrality	1	1	2		
	Homogeneity	1		2		1
	Separability			2		
	Logic/ Implementation Errors; Fallibility			2		
	Design Sensitivity/ Fragility/Limits/ Finiteness			2		
	Unrecoverability			1		
Behavior	Behavioral Sensitivity /Fragility			2		
	Malevolence			2		
	Rigidity			2		
	Malleability			2		
	Gullibility/ Deceivability/Naiveté	1	1	2		1
	Complacency			2		
	Corruptibility/ Controllability	1	1	2		1
General	Accessible/ Detectable/ Identifiable/ Transparent/ Interceptable	2	2	2		2
	Hard to Manage or Control	1	1	1		
	Self Unawareness and Unpredictability			1	2	
	Predictability	2				1

General management. Ensure that procedures are in place (e.g., security campaigns and reminders) to alert staff of the dangers of insider threats (including their own unwitting recruitment) and other threats to critical information systems.

Self-awareness, monitoring, and assessments. (See "Attack detection . . . " below. Consider especially the use of intrusion detection software within the local area networks [LANs].)

Deception for intelligence, surveillance, and reconnaissance. Create "honeypots" (e.g., files containing bogus but attractive information) within critical systems so that accessing these honeypots will generate an alert stating that an individual is engaging in suspicious behavior and should be monitored.

Attack detection, recognition, damage assessment, and forensics (self and foe). Consider the use of real-time "intrusion detection" software to detect abnormal behavior that violates a set of preprogrammed rules or exhibits statistical abnormalities. Review access and audit logs for suspicious behavior.

Unpredictable to adversary. Limit knowledge of system configurations, key component locations, and key system dependencies—even within "trusted" staff.

Deterrence. Use criminal and legal penalties (see below) against offenders to deter others.

Criminal and legal penalties and guarantees. Ensure that criminal and legal penalties for insider attacks are well developed, used when appropriate, and thus act as a deterrence.

Law enforcement, civil proceedings. Use law enforcement to punish illegal behavior as a deterrence.

Inability to Handle Distributed Denial-of-Service Attacks

Vulnerability Attribute: Behavioral sensitivity/fragility.

Type of Target: Cyber.

One of the most difficult kinds of cyber attack to handle is a DDoS attack, wherein hundreds or thousands of different computers bombard a specific network router or other component with packets or requests for service—usually ones with erroneous information that require additional time for processing. Information networks must be especially configured and designed if they are to thwart (to the extent possible) this kind of attack that depends on behavioral characteristics and sensitivities of the network(s).

Potential Relevant Mitigation Strategies:

Decentralization. Consider using parallel or backup servers that can take over when the primary server is incapacitated due to a DDoS attack. Use rotating server responsibilities to present an unpredictable moving target to the DDoS attacker.

VV&A, software/hardware engineering, evaluations, testing. Test the network (e.g., through "red teaming" and other means) for robustness against DDoS attacks.

Control of exposure, access, and output. Establish control points at various positions in the network where filters can be installed for DDoS traffic.

Fault, uncertainty, validity, and quality tolerance and graceful degradation. Consider means to allow graceful degradation of the networks under DDoS attack (e.g., by reducing all other IP traffic from other applications).

Dynamic resource allocation. Provide a rapid way to cut off DDoS traffic further up the network chain (e.g., at the gateway to your Internet service provider).

Self-awareness, monitoring, and assessments. Provide monitoring for early warning of DDoS attacks at all levels of gateways within critical IP networks; have preplanned procedures in place for reaction when such monitoring detects a DDoS attack.

IP Spoofing

Vulnerability Attribute: Gullibility/deceivability/naiveté.

Type of Target: Cyber.

To "spoof" an IP address, within a packet or message, means to substitute an erroneous address in the place where a valid one should appear. By this means, it becomes difficult to ascertain the true sender of an information packet or session, and therefore difficult to permit various forms of attack that disguise their source.

Potential Relevant Mitigation Strategies:

Hardening; also *control of exposure, access, and output.* Consider enforcing various firewall precautions and rules—for example, disallowing any IP packets to be emitted from a local network with source IP addresses not valid for that network.

Threat response structures and plans. When any host (computer) in the system determines that invalid IP addresses are being used by some sender, a preplanned response can be initiated to alert other hosts to block transmissions from the addresses.

Adaptability and learning. Firewalls, routers, and other devices operating key IP networks may be adaptable so that responses to known IP-spoofing attacks can be quickly instituted throughout the network.

Vaccination. (See "Threat response structures and plans" above.) As soon as a bogus IP address is discovered, other hosts and routers in the network could be "vaccinated" against it, as a rudimentary form of "immunological defense system."

Self-awareness, monitoring, and assessments. Firewalls, routers, and similar devices must constantly be alert to bogus IP addresses so that remedial steps such as those above can be taken.

Inability to Detect Changes to IP Net, Making IP Masking Possible

Vulnerability Attribute: Self-unawareness and unpredictability.

Type of Target: Cyber.

If an IP network does not have active monitoring programs and tools to allow personnel to ascertain whether a new host (IP address) has been inserted, or removed, from the net, then it could be possible for someone to insert an unauthorized laptop or another device onto a network connection and download information into that device. This danger is especially prevalent for wireless networks, where the "connection" can be from a location away from visible network ports or even outside the organization's building. This is a lack of "self-awareness" of the network configuration, and changes to it, during its operation.

Potential Relevant Mitigation Strategies:

Centralization. Institute a central, real-time network monitoring activity, with sensors and application programs capable of detecting and displaying any changes to the network configuration.

Self-awareness, monitoring, and assessments. Through appropriate monitoring tools and techniques, the network should be aware of any changes to its configuration, and highlight those—at the time they occur—in a display or signal to network operators.

Centralized Network Operations Centers

Vulnerability Attribute: Centrality.

Type of Target: Physical.

Network operations centers can contain many vital physical components (e.g., key equipment and backups) in one central location. As such, a physical attack could disable not only primary, but also backup, routers and key communications equipment.

Potential Relevant Mitigation Strategies:

Decentralization. Consider providing multiple support centers. Do not store backup equipment in the same physical location as main equipment. Provide multiple access points where routers can be placed on the physical LAN cables.

Control of exposure, access, and output. Restrict physical access to the room based on need-to-use. Provide protective shielding or structure (physical and electrical) to help prevent accidental or deliberate changes, damage, etc. Put tamper-resistant tabs on the panel and/or shielding. Keep backup equipment off-line to provide protection until needed.

Hardening. Provide protective shielding or structure (physical and electrical) to help prevent accidental or deliberate changes, damage, etc. Put tamper-resistant tabs on the panel and/or shielding. Keep backup equipment off-line to provide protection until needed.

Threat response structures and plans. Have preplanned procedures for recovery to any centralized components.

Rapid reconstitution and recovery. Generate plans on how to manually rebuild capability for vital communications. Develop replacement contingencies. Examine local ability to repair systems. Store backup equipment and configuration information in a different location that is not likely to be destroyed in the same physical attack.

Common Commercial Software and Hardware Are Well Known and Predictable

Vulnerability Attribute: Predictability.

Type of Target: Physical and Cyber.

The personal computers, workstations, routers, servers, and other components of critical information systems are often heavily based on commercial products, such as Cisco router software; Windows NT; Microsoft Outlook, Word, Excel, PowerPoint, etc. As such, the vulnerabilities, organization, and, in some cases, source code of such programs are widely known. These programs are thus highly predictable in that other copies of them can be tested to find situations (e.g., exceeding the capacity of a database) in which their performance fails.

Potential Relevant Mitigation Strategies:

Heterogeneity. Consider using a variety of COTS software and hardware—for example, Netscape in addition to Internet Explorer; Netscape mail in addition to Microsoft Outlook. Then a virus or worm capitalizing on a well-known flaw may not infect all systems at the same time.

VV&A, software/hardware engineering, evaluations, testing. To the extent possible, test heavily used commercial hardware and software in critical information systems for vulnerabilities. Use "red team" approaches to system testing. Use "open source" code for critical operating systems and applications that can be inspected for buried flaws. (Note that the many users in the open-source community already search for such flaws and use of seasoned open-source code inherits the benefits of their labors.)

Management. Ensure that any available patches and fixes are tested and installed rapidly as soon as they become available.

Immunological defense systems. Establish protocols to rapidly share information on an attack's reliance on standard commercial-system vulnerabilities and configurations.

Deception for counterintelligence. Provide deceptive files (e.g., WIN file types on UNIX and Macintosh equipment and software) to make it harder to determine the type of software being used, especially via automatic scanning programs. Place system files in unorthodox places or store them under different names (e.g., do not store UNIX binaries under /bin; do not store system files under "C:WINNT" or "C:Program Files"; change the default folder name for email attachments).

Unpredictable to adversary. Remove information about the type of software used from both internally and externally accessible systems when possible.

Standardized Software

Vulnerability Attribute: Homogeneity.

Type of Target: Cyber.

The heavy use of standardized software for routers (e.g., Cisco operating system), servers (e.g., Windows NT), and PCs/workstations (e.g., Windows NT or Macintosh OS) creates a very homogeneous information and communication system. Any flaw in one of these designs can be replicated widely within the information system and therefore can provide a common vulnerability across the system.

Potential Relevant Mitigation Strategies:

Heterogeneity. Consider deliberate use of alternative software (e.g., Linux, Macintosh OS, Sun Solaris) as part of the network or desktop configuration so that if any virus, worm, or other cyberattack "takes down" all standard systems (e.g., Windows NT running Outlook), then these other systems may continue operating and provide emergency service until the damage is contained, isolated, and removed.

VV&A, software/hardware engineering, evaluations, testing. To the extent that standardized (homogeneous) system components are widely used throughout critical systems, use extra testing to ensure they are free of exploitable flaws to the extent possible.

Hardening. Dependence on standardized software should trigger extra measures to ensure that it is "hardened" against attack—for example, by retaining backup copies of critical operating systems and applications in a "hard" (unmodifiable) medium, such as CD-ROM or DVD-R, for use in recovering systems after an attack.

Fault, uncertainty, validity, and quality tolerance and graceful degradation. Ensure that standardized software is "fault tolerant" and degrades gracefully under various types of attacks. For example, software might shed noncritical applications when an attack is sensed and shut various firewall options to help thwart a cyberattack.

Weaknesses in Router or Desktop Applications Software

Vulnerability Attribute: Logic/implementation errors; fallibility.

Type of Target: Cyber.

Fundamental design or implementation flaws in standard software used in operating systems (workstation and router) and desktop applications may exist. These flaws, if they become known to an attacker, could provide unauthorized access or destruction.

Potential Relevant Mitigation Strategies:

Heterogeneity. Use a diverse set of servers based on differing software (such as email programs) and operating systems (e.g., UNIX in addition to Windows NT), especially on systems with higher security standards.

VV&A, software/hardware engineering, evaluations, testing. Conduct thorough "red teaming" and testing of COTS products to understand inherent vulnerabilities; develop security procedures to mitigate vulnerabilities. Ensure proper firewall installations and maintenance at boundaries as well as locally (when feasible). Keep up to date on patches and fixes as they become available.

Control of exposure, access, and output. Restrict physical access to key equipment based on need-to-use, helping to prevent insider or intruder cyber attacks and accidents.

General management. Ensure that all procedures to protect "root" access are implemented and kept up to date.

Immunological defense systems. Adopt "immunological" defensive measures, in which one system, detecting an attack or flaw, notifies other similar systems to increase their defenses against such an attack or flaw.

Vaccination. Have a central location automatically "vaccinate" systemwide components and computers with patches and fixes as soon as they become tested and available. Be careful that this centralized updating procedure is well protected to prevent an easy target for spreading attacks across the information system and that patches and fixes are well tested.

Electronic Environmental Tolerances

Vulnerability Attribute: Design sensitivity/fragility/limits/finiteness.

Type of Target: Physical.

Various commercial electronic equipment vital to network communications and computing are often not hardened for environmental influences (e.g., temperature, smoke, humidity) or extreme attack means (e.g., EMPs).

Potential Relevant Mitigation Strategies:

Heterogeneity. Consider using equipment with differing ranges of environmental tolerances, so entire capabilities would not be lost under certain extreme environmental conditions.

Redundancy. Store backup equipment in sealed containers, perhaps with EMP-shielding. Provide local, redundant environmental conditioning equipment for singular, centralized equipment rooms.

VV&A, software/hardware engineering, evaluations, testing. Test and make available the environmental ranges within which key electronic equipment can operate; attempt to procure equipment with the least environmental sensitivity.

Control of exposure, access, and output. Install positive pressure air conditioning to keep smoke, humidity, or other environmental hazards from entering electronic environments—especially those with singularities. Install EMP shielding for critical equipment and for a subset of terminals that can be used for minimal capability under adverse conditions.

Hardening. (See "Install EMP shielding . . . " and "Store backup equipment in sealed containers . . . " above.)

Self-awareness, monitoring, and assessments. Install sensors for all adverse environmental conditions that could affect electronic equipment, especially those that are singular or centralized. Have prearranged contingency plans for when environmental conditions exceed those under which the equipment can operate.

Chapter Seven

AUTOMATING AND EXECUTING THE METHODOLOGY: A SPREADSHEET TOOL

Manually working through the evolved methodology's large matrix, evaluator filters, and attack-component filters is laborious for an evaluator and may prevent thorough or careful application of the VAM methodology. Moreover, looking up the definitions of the various vulnerabilities, security techniques, and attack methods during the course of an evaluation can be daunting as well. Therefore, a prototype computerized tool has been developed and implemented to assist in using the methodology. This tool is implemented as a Microsoft Excel spreadsheet using Visual Basic algorithms to perform information lookups as well as simple scoring of vulnerability risks based on the inputs from the evaluator.[1]

Even with this tool, it is important to realize that comprehensive vulnerability assessments cannot be fully automated. Automated network and computer scanning software and methodologies can identify specific, known vulnerabilities such as back doors, open ports, missing patches, throughput limitations, operating anomalies, and the like. However, automated tools cannot conduct a top-down review of properties that have yet to be exploited or which involve the full range of physical, human/social, and infrastructure configurations and behaviors. Their fidelity depends greatly on the breadth of their threat or operating models, the inputs they generate, and the outputs they observe. Comprehensive reviews often require the deep knowledge and experience of people intimately involved in the information system and its operations. Our methodology is an aid to evaluators, yet the automated tool helps the evaluator deal with the large amount of information in the methodology.

INITIAL STEPS PERFORMED MANUALLY

Steps 1 and 2 of the methodology (identifying the critical information functions and identifying the critical information systems supporting these functions) are executed manually through evaluator assessments and reviews of the information system in question. Although complex in their own right, these two steps often require

[1]Nothing inherent about Excel's functionality was required to implement the prototype tool. It was chosen simply as a convenient and commonly available spreadsheet application in which the required algorithms could be implemented. A Web-based tool might be another useful platform for implementing the tool, given its ease of access and availability (see Chapter Eight).

organizational investigations and considerations of those that are hard to structure and facilitate with a small tool. Such processes as OCTAVE (Alberts et al., 1999, 2001) have forms and procedures that can be considered for these steps, and the Common Criteria (ISO 15408) specifies a breadth of issues and considerations that should be addressed by selected processes.

VULNERABILITIES GUIDED BY AND RECORDED ON A FORM

For step 3, a worksheet form is available in the VAM tool (see Table 4.2). This worksheet should be completed for each information system (or major subsystem) under review and at various architectural levels within the system. This form facilitates the execution of step 3 of the methodology (identifying the vulnerabilities in the critical systems) by providing the evaluator with the full list of vulnerability properties in the rows and listing the four different object types in an information system (physical, cyber, human/social, and infrastructure) as columns. Using this form helps to ensure a broad review of target vulnerabilities across all these dimensions rather than a simple recording of the standard types of vulnerabilities that come to mind or those that are commonly raised in the evaluator's organization.

Remember also that the vulnerability to security technique matrix identifies cautions when security techniques may incur vulnerabilities. The evaluator may find it useful to work through that matrix (either manually in Table 6.1 or using the Excel tool described below) to see what vulnerabilities may already be present in the system as a result of the security techniques employed.

THE RISK ASSESSMENT AND MITIGATION SELECTION SPREADSHEET

After performing the first three steps, the methodology's complexity increases greatly. The vulnerability assessment and mitigation selection spreadsheet shown in Figure 7.1 reduces this complexity by providing automated lookups and calculations based on both the methodology and the information supplied by the evaluator.

Specifying the User Type and Vulnerability to Be Analyzed

First, the evaluator sets up the basic information for the vulnerability as shown in Figure 7.2. The evaluator's job role is provided at part 1, specifying which evaluator role filter to employ in the analysis on the form. A free text box is included at part 2 to allow the user to describe the vulnerability under study (i.e., copying and embellishing the description noted on the vulnerability form). Parts 3 and 4 specify the type of vulnerability property and type of object under question as pull-down menus.

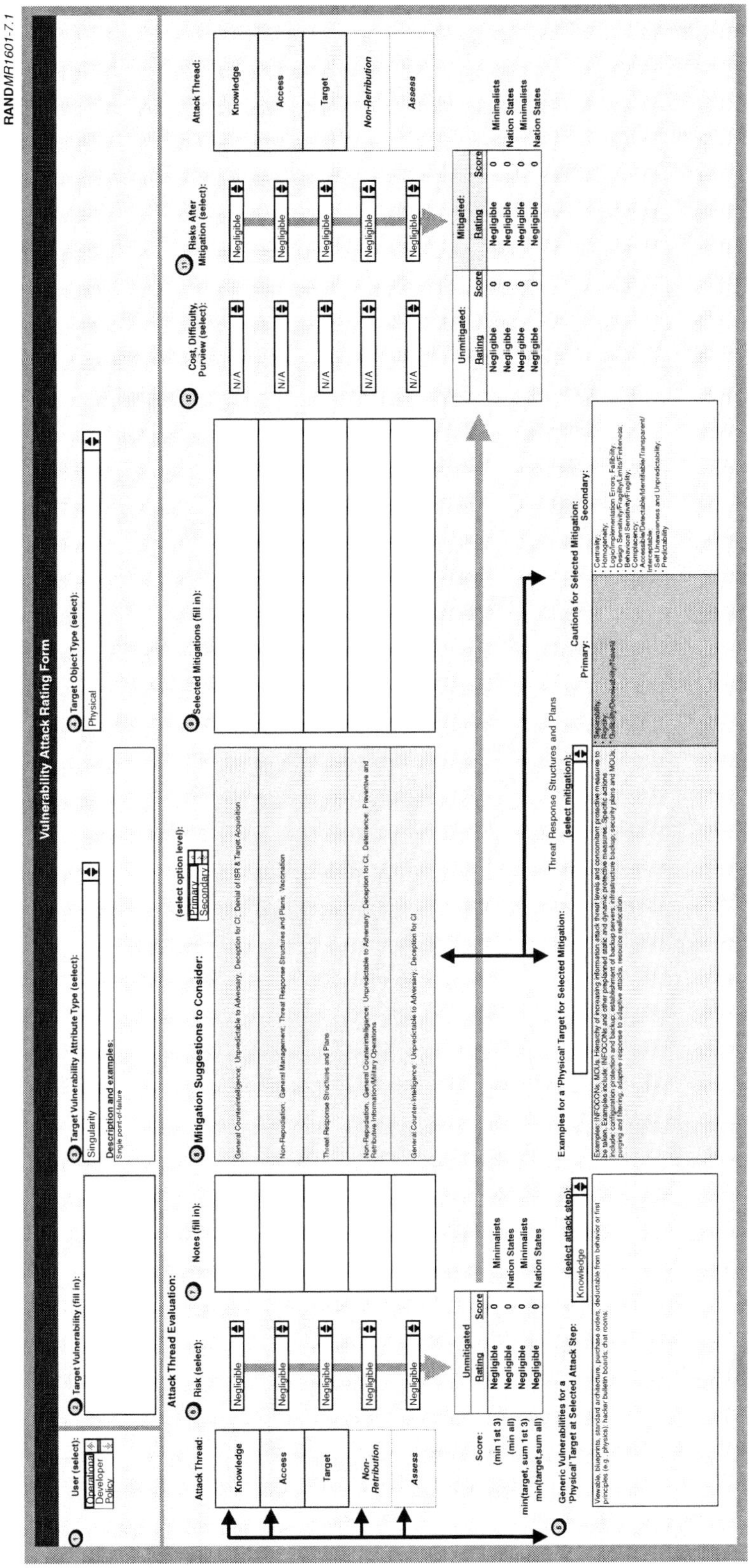

Figure 7.1—The VAM Methodology Spreadsheet Tool

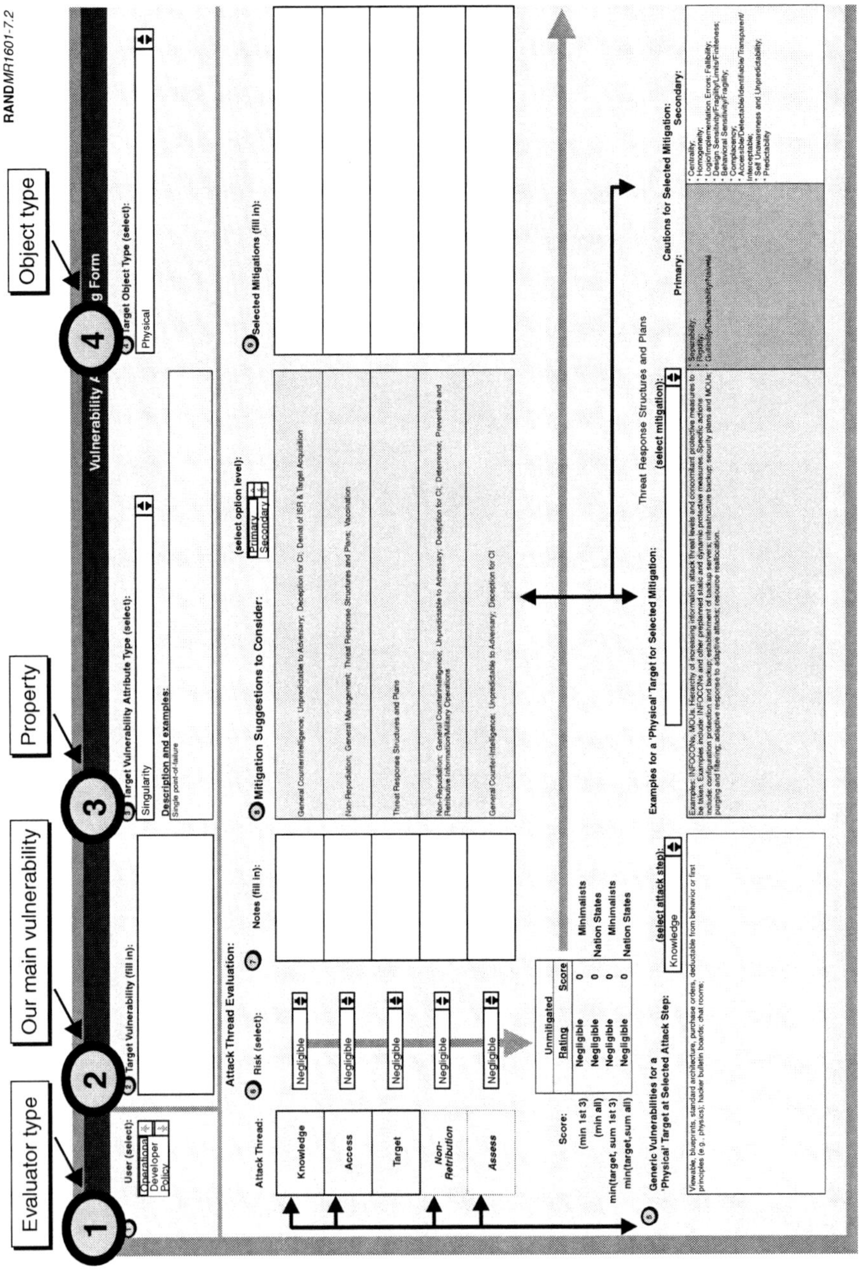

Figure 7.2—Specifying the User Type and Vulnerability to Be Analyzed

Evaluating the Risks for Each Attack Component

Second, the evaluator needs to evaluate the risks of the system vulnerability for the five attack components—knowledge, access, target vulnerability, non-retribution, and assess—by completing steps 5 through 7, shown in Figure 7.3. Nondeliberate failures can be assessed by completing only the target vulnerability row with the vulnerability that leads to the failure of concern.

Part 5 allows the evaluator to review the basic ways an adversary may achieve the four supporting attack components (knowledge, access, non-retribution, and assess) that support the target vulnerability assessed earlier in step 3. Here the evaluator can select an attack component in the pull-down menu and view the methods from Table 6.4 based on the object type specified in part 4.

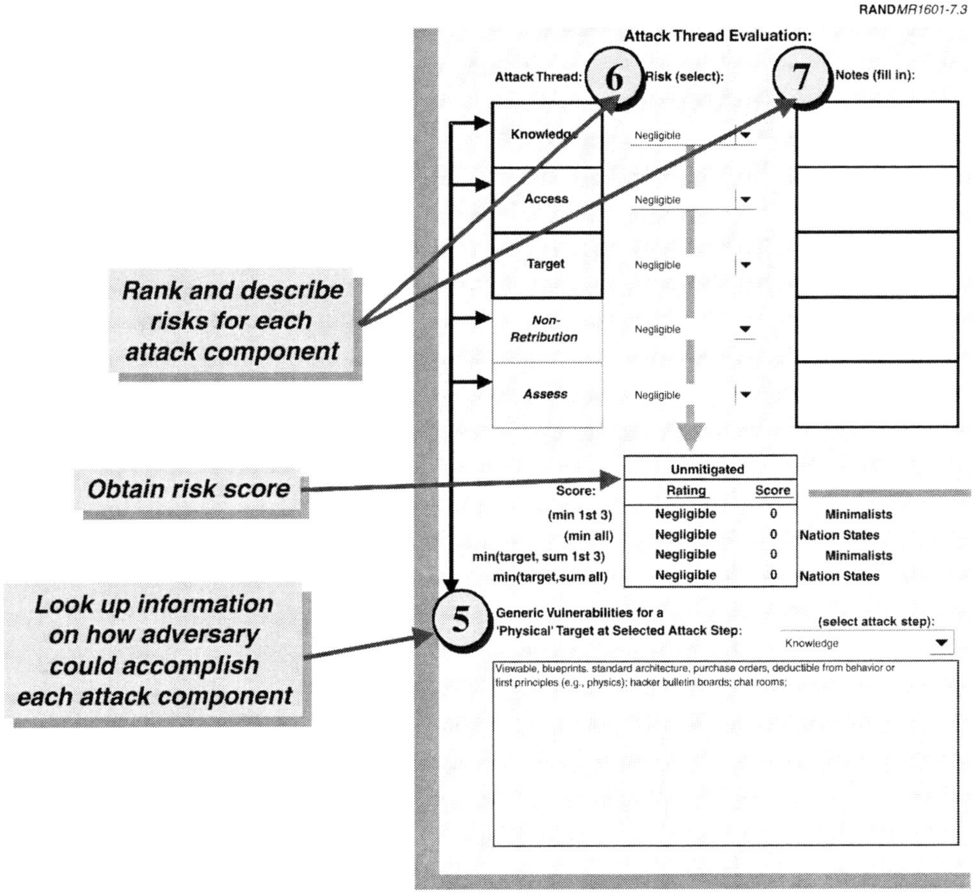

Figure 7.3—Evaluating the Risks for Each Attack Component

Based on prior reviews and part 5, the evaluator rates in step 6 the risks for each of the five attack components using pull-down menus. The risks are rated as either *negligible, low, moderate,* or *high.*

Based on these ratings, the system performs four simple calculations to provide a combined risk rating and score. The risk rating gives a simple *negligible, low, moderate,* or *high* value for all five components together, while the score is a numeric value between 0 and 10. The tool uses four simple algorithms to combine the risk ratings.

The first algorithm, labeled "min 1st 3," uses the minimum rating from the key three attack components (knowledge, access, and target vulnerability) that are essential to any IO/IW attack. This algorithm takes the philosophy of rating the "weakest link" of the essential components and is most relevant to mitigation strategies that try to prevent an attack by denying the adversary a key link in the attack (e.g., when dealing with minimalist attackers who do not worry as much about non-retribution or assessing the success of their attack).

The second algorithm, labeled "min all," also uses the "weakest link" philosophy but provides the minimum rating from all five attack components. Thus, this value is most relevant in situations in which the adversary is concerned with all five components equally (e.g., nation-states) and in which the security approach is to deny the attacker all these links.

The third algorithm, labeled "min(target, sum 1st 3)," calculates a combined rating of the three key components but chooses the target rating if it is less than that combined sum. This algorithm is useful when the evaluator, in dealing with minimalist attackers, wants to combine the values of the key components but also recognizes that the target vulnerability is essential (i.e., if there is a very low risk to the target vulnerability, no amount of knowledge or access will improve the ultimate attackability of the target).

Finally the fourth algorithm, labeled "min(target, sum all)," combines all five attack components (i.e., for nation-state attacks) but also recognizes that the target vulnerability has to be there for an attack.

Other algorithms could, of course, be developed to combine the evaluator-supplied risk ratings, but these four serve as reasonable starting points in trying to provide an overall rating for the vulnerability in question. The use of the "min" function reflects the importance of each component to an information attack (sometimes reflected in the saying that "IO is a three-legged stool"), and the resulting important security observation that even though a user may not be able to address a vulnerability in one area (say, the target vulnerability from a computer design), techniques applied in other areas (say, denying access or knowledge) can have a significant positive effect in securing a system. The "sum" function can also be useful in combining mitigation effects across the attack components, especially when complete risk mitigation is not possible in a key area.

Additional use of these score-combination algorithms is needed to understand their utility and validity under different types of attack weightings and approaches for different adversary types. Given the subjective nature of the ratings, more-complicated algorithms may be meaningless and merely make it harder to understand the underlying risks. Under certain circumstances, it may be beneficial merely to compare the pre- and post-mitigated ratings input by the user, forgoing the scoring mechanism.

Tool users will note that the system provides colorings to the ratings (clear, yellow, orange, and red, respectively) to improve the ability to skim the ratings on the spreadsheet and quickly determine how a given vulnerability rates (especially in comparison to ratings for other vulnerabilities on separate worksheets), how effective the mitigation strategies are anticipated to be, and what attack components will receive the mitigation focus.

Considering and Selecting Mitigations

Third, the evaluator uses the tool to review and select mitigation strategies across the attack component areas. Figure 7.4 shows the part of the spreadsheet that automates the matrix lookup, matching relevant security techniques to vulnerabilities for each attack component given the evaluator's role.

RANDMR1601-7.4

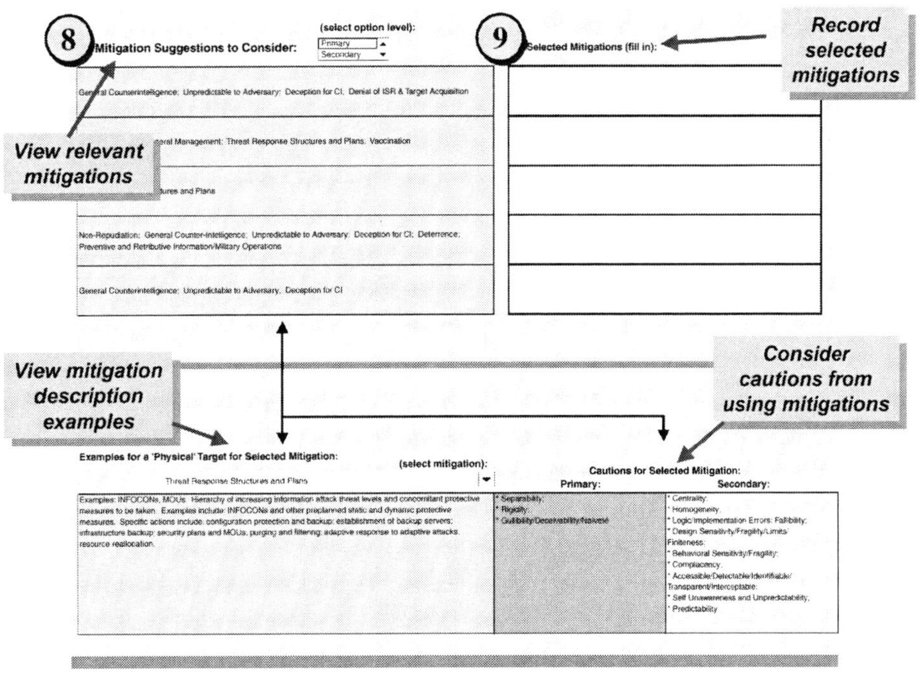

Figure 7.4—Considering and Selecting Mitigations

Part 8 allows the evaluator to review the mitigation recommendations for each of the attack components. The primary or secondary recommendations from the matrix are shown based on the evaluator's selection in the list menu. Relevant techniques are shown in the five attack category rows. Examples and explanations of what these techniques entail can be viewed by selecting the technique in the pull-down menu below the suggestion list. The tool also looks up the primary and secondary cautions in the matrix for the indicated security technique.

Using this information, the evaluator selects the best mitigation approaches for his or her particular situation, taking into account the cautions, the risk profile across the attack components, the available techniques across that profile, the implementation issues (cost, availability, purview, etc.), and the potential benefits. Part 9 provides free text space for the evaluator to record the security techniques he or she plans to implement.

Rating Costs and the Mitigated Risks

Now that the evaluator has selected the security techniques for further consideration and implementation, the tool allows the evaluator to record his or her rating of the cost, difficulty, and purview for each attack component's mitigation set under part 10 in Figure 7.5.

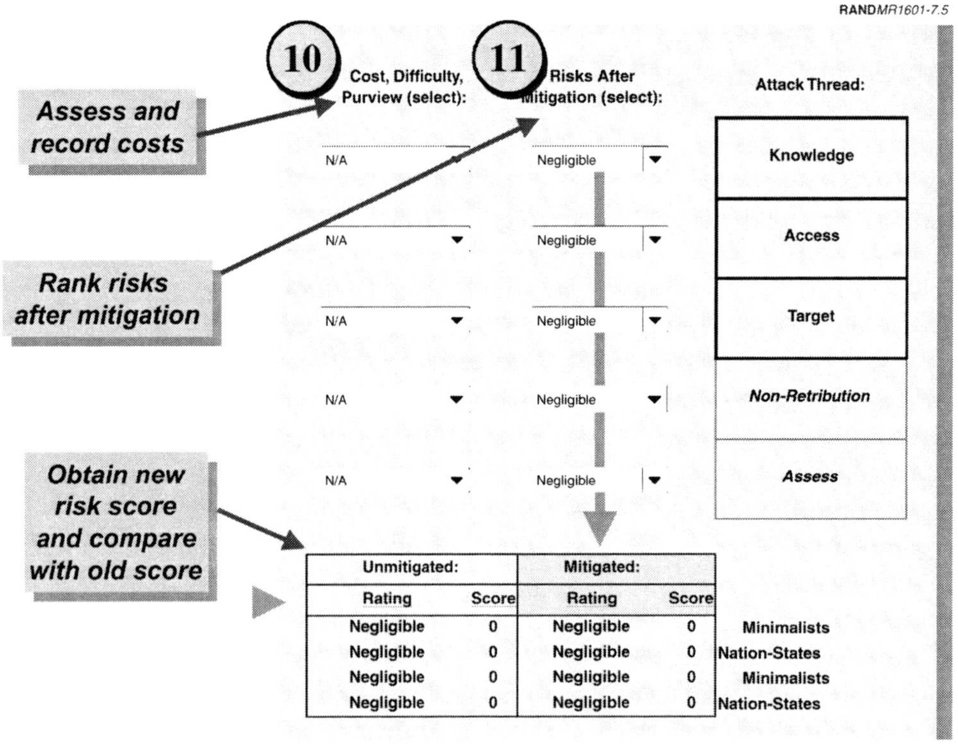

Figure 7.5—Rating Costs and the Mitigated Risks

This figure also shows part 11, where the evaluator can estimate what the risks should be for each component of the attack after the selected security techniques are implemented. The mitigated risk estimates use the same format as the unmitigated risk rating scheme, employing pull-down menus and four rating values (negligible, low, moderate, or high). The tool uses the same algorithms to produce combined risk ratings and scores, and shows again the unmitigated ratings and scores next to the new ones for comparison.

In addition to helping the evaluator work through estimates and decide which security techniques to pursue, the cost, applicability, and risk ratings help to record these assessments for future review. They provide a visual representation of the evaluator's expert assessments both when reviewing the security techniques under consideration for all the vulnerabilities across each worksheet completed and to provide descriptions and overviews to managers and customers for approval and funding decisions.

The evaluator can also use parts 10 and 11 in the worksheet to record the results of applying and testing the security techniques to the actual system (steps 5 and 6 of the methodology). These results are much more definitive than the evaluator's estimates during step 4 and are important to record both to reassess what additional procedures should be taken to mitigate the identified (i.e., a repeat of steps 4–6) and for future reference in rating the effect of security techniques in reducing risks.

Chapter Eight

NEXT STEPS AND DISCUSSION

Here we present some deficiencies in the current VAM methodology, possible next steps, and some general discussion about the methodology, its use, and the utility of security assessments.

FUTURE CHALLENGES AND OPPORTUNITIES

While the VAM methodology advances the techniques available for assessing and mitigating information system vulnerabilities, the entire six-step methodology would benefit from additional automation development and support aids.

Guiding the Evaluation of Critical Functions and Systems

Applying the *strategy-to-tasks* technique to reviewing the critical information functions and their supporting systems (steps 1 and 2) may benefit from specific guidance and worksheets in the tool to help the evaluator explore what is most critical and to help prompt an objective review that avoids standard concerns and predefined notions. These steps focus on the essential information functions and the systems essential for supporting the functions, but additional thought or structure may be helpful for addressing and relating the so-called *valuable* functions and systems, as well as the essential functions and systems.

Additional Guidance and Automation: Spreadsheet and Web-Based Implementations

While the current spreadsheet tool greatly assists in exercising the methodology (especially steps 3 and 4), the use of a Web-based implementation could offer a number of significant advantages. A Web-based version could be structured around a question-and-answer format, in which the system helps walk the evaluator through the entire process. The system could also help the evaluator deal with the complexity of multiple vulnerabilities by automatically filling in subordinate forms with prior data and settings. An online database could also facilitate the storage and preservation of the assessment findings and eliminate the need to duplicate worksheet forms for multiple vulnerability assessments. Nevertheless, the spreadsheet version has proven very useful in our early application of the methodology to Naval systems, and we anticipate receiving feedback from additional users who have shown interest in using the methodology.

Prioritizing Security Options

The method of deciding what security techniques to employ and how well they cover the vulnerability space can also benefit from additional operational mathematics. An unpublished approach developed by Richard Hillestad and colleagues at RAND has been used as a complement to the VAM methodology in reviewing RAND's own organizational vulnerabilities, generating security options, and prioritizing these options given fiscal constraints and the organization's risk tolerance. We anticipate that this integer programming-based approach will be useful to other organizations and will serve an important complementary role with the VAM methodology.

Quantitative Assessments of Threats, Risks, and Mitigations

Quantitative assessments and valuations of threats, risks, and mitigations remain a challenge. The simple assessments currently used in the methodology rely on the subjective expertise of the evaluator and do not provide an independent way to generate quantitative (or even qualitative) values. This problem is exacerbated in the areas where the VAM methodology shines: when the threats are theoretical and when vulnerabilities have yet to be exploited by adversaries. If there is no history of attacks, then it is hard to

- estimate a probability that the vulnerability will be exploited,
- perform a cost-benefit analysis for security investments against that threat, or
- conduct tradeoff analysis between various theoretical threats and vulnerabilities.

This problem was poignantly demonstrated in the difficulties of justifying counterterrorism funding before the attacks of September 11, 2001, and in calculating the probability and severity of anthrax attacks before the anthrax mailings in 2002. However, September 11 and the anthrax mailings demonstrated the importance of finding and mitigating previously unexploited vulnerabilities and continuing to look for the next vulnerability that an adversary may turn to once one addresses a previously exploited vulnerability. We need to be proactive in addition to reactive.

Integrating VAM Functions into Other Assessment Methodologies

Given that many security assessment methodologies share very similar steps with the VAM methodology's six steps and the fact that many of these methodologies lack the depth of VAM's assessment and mitigation suggestion, it may be useful to use the core of VAM (steps 3 and 4) during the execution of these other established methodologies and/or formally integrating VAM's core vulnerabilities, matrix, filtering, and supporting information into these methods.

Using VAM to Guide Information Attacks

The primary focus of the methodology to date has been in information system protection, but the broader review of vulnerability fundamentals and attack stages could be useful in understanding IO/IW. A comprehensive review of what a defender may do before, during, or after an attack in response to our own attack can also help us to design more effective IO tools, methods, and procedures while minimizing our exposure.

Applications of VAM Beyond Information Systems

In addition, the explicit handling of physical, human/social, and infrastructure systems raises the possibility that the methodology may be useful in assessing and mitigating vulnerabilities in systems other than information systems. Many types of systems that are critical to social functions (e.g., financial, power, transportation, agricultural, water, medical, law enforcement, governance) rely on physical, human/social, and infrastructure objects and include growing dependence on cyber components. RAND has not yet explored the issues in expanding the application of the methodology to these domains, but these opportunities seem promising. The list of vulnerability properties and number of critical attack components may need to be expanded in some of these domains (e.g., in the biological domain), but many of the fundamental properties and attack stages will likely be applicable and useful to consider.

WHAT VULNERABILITY WILL FAIL OR BE ATTACKED NEXT?

One of the methodology's strong points is the ability to help the evaluator think "out of the box" and look for new vulnerabilities that have yet to cause system failures or be exploited by attackers. This kind of review can be quite important when the system is complex or the adversary is creative and adaptive to the security responses and postures used by the defender. For example, robustness through redundancy or performance monitoring can be important as organizations come to rely more on complex information systems. Also, terrorist organizations tend to look for simple yet easy vulnerabilities to exploit, while current security procedures often focus on solving yesterday's exploited vulnerability.

USABILITY ISSUES

Note that even if the evaluator cannot directly fix a vulnerability by implementing the security techniques, the assessment can nevertheless be useful in providing a comprehensive justification and explanation of the vulnerability to other individuals who do have the responsibility and authority to implement remedies to the vulnerability. Such assessments and justifications can be quite important in informing others of the security needs and providing a basis for management budgeting and decision-making.

Note also that little discussion has been included here on how to implement specific security techniques or on testing the effectiveness of the security techniques. Such testing as red teaming and actual attack exercises can be difficult to accomplish. Oftentimes, an organization is too busy conducting operations to run an exercise that can take down its critical information systems. INFOCONs, for example, are usually simulated during attack exercises, and aggressive red teaming is rarely conducted against real operational systems. Also, standard certification for military deployments (e.g., inspections, certifications, assessments, and visits [ICAV], such as a Computer Network Vulnerability Assessment) runs through bottom-up vulnerabilities (patches, alerts, viruses, etc.) with little creative red teaming. Anderson et al. (1999) includes additional thoughts on steps 5 and 6.

WHY PERFORM SECURITY ASSESSMENTS?

Performing a security assessment can require significant investment in time and resources, but you get what you pay for. These investments might be viewed by some as unnecessary, since many vulnerabilities are known and because limited resources may already prevent the implementation of security responses to the vulnerabilities. Thus, many may not see a market for comprehensive assessments or for discovering vulnerabilities that have not yet been exploited by adversaries.

This position is shortsighted. A careful, objective review of security problems can help justify additional expenditures. The execution of a methodology like VAM links security investments to vulnerabilities to critical information functions, allowing management to better understand the operational significance of vulnerabilities. Thus, the justifications for resource requests are expressed in the proper language and level of functional effects rather than as mere wish lists with indeterminate effects on the core functions of an organization.

Also, executing a methodology can help to balance limited resources, ensuring that the most important vulnerabilities are fixed first and that alternative security techniques with better cost-benefit ratios are not overlooked.

Chapter Nine

SUMMARY AND CONCLUSIONS

VAM fills a gap in existing methodologies by providing explicit guidance on finding system vulnerabilities and by suggesting relevant mitigations. The VAM methodology provides a comprehensive, top-down approach to information system security, combining a novel assessment and recommendation-generating matrix with filtering approaches to refine the security options under consideration.

The methodology helps to identify new types of vulnerabilities as well as known types of vulnerabilities in one's information systems. Thus, the methodology takes a comprehensive approach to understanding vulnerabilities and does not rely on canned scanning tools or checklists (however valuable) for the sole identifier of vulnerabilities of concern.

The vulnerabilities and security taxonomies in the methodology are fairly complete. Viewing vulnerability properties separate from system objects has proved a valuable way of reviewing the system for vulnerabilities, since the properties often apply to each type of object. Also, each object type plays important roles in information systems. The realization and expansion of the vulnerability review to explicitly consider physical, human/social, and infrastructure objects in addition to cyber and computer hardware objects recognize and accommodate the importance of all these aspects to the proper functioning of information systems.

Providing a computerized aid that executes the methodology during an evaluation greatly improved the usability of the methodology, especially given that the current approach generates many more suggestions than the earlier version by Anderson et al. (1999).

The current spreadsheet implementation in Excel has the benefit of being usable by the large number of personal computer users that already have the Excel program on their machines. The spreadsheet also gives the user flexibility to generate analysis reports and even input custom rating algorithms to accommodate local needs and situations.

The methodology can be used to improve security both during system design stages and during operation. The methodology also identifies steps that policymakers can make to improve information system security.

The methodology should be useful for individuals and teams. Individuals can focus on their individual situation and areas of responsibility, while teams can bring multiple expertises to bear on the analyses as well as perspectives on different divisions within an organization. The methodology could also be used in parallel by different divisions to focus on their own vulnerabilities, integrating them later at a high-level review once each group's needs and justifications are understood. While the VAM methodology has proven its worth in separate studies of real information systems, the current methodology would benefit from additional development of guidance for steps 1 and 2 and tool automation refinement. Integration with identified techniques that aid in the analysis of risks and the cost-effectiveness of security options would be useful and is being pursued.

We also believe that the general approach of the methodology, as well as a significant portion of the vulnerability attributes, could be extended to other systems whose primary role is not information processing. We are also exploring these possibilities.

VULNERABILITY TO MITIGATION MAP VALUES

The core of our methodology is the matrix of values that maps vulnerability attributes to the security techniques that can mitigate these vulnerabilities (Table 6.1). In the tables below we list and explain why certain techniques can be useful in mitigating each vulnerability attribute. We also call attention to instances in which certain mitigation techniques can incur vulnerabilities.

Each table lists the security techniques that appear most relevant for the table's vulnerability attribute. The security techniques are listed in the left columns and descriptions of why each security technique was deemed relevant is listed in the right columns. Furthermore, the security techniques are grouped according to whether they were judged to be of *primary* and common importance in helping to mitigate the vulnerability attribute, or of *secondary* and less common importance. As described in Chapter Six, primary techniques are identified with a numeral *2* in Table 6.1, and secondary techniques are identified with a numeral *1*. Some tables here also contain security techniques that can be *facilitated* by the table's vulnerability. When present, these techniques are listed in the last rows and are identified with a numeral *0* in Table 6.1.

So, for example, Table A.1 lists Heterogeneity as a primary mitigation technique for the Singularity vulnerability attribute, and Centralization as a secondary technique. Table 6.1, therefore, has a *2* at the intersection of the Singularity attribute and the technique Heterogeneity, and a *1* at the intersection of the Singularity attribute and the technique Centralization. No security techniques are identified as being facilitated by singularities. Table A.3, however, identifies four security techniques (Centralization, Adaptability and Learning, Deception for ISR, and Law Enforcement and Civil Proceedings) that are facilitated by the Centrality vulnerability attribute. Each techniques has a *0* in the Centrality row in Table 6.1.

MITIGATION TECHNIQUES THAT ADDRESS OR ARE FACILITATED BY VULNERABILITIES

Table A.1

Mitigation Techniques That Address Singularity

Primary	
Heterogeneity	Heterogeneity provides alternatives to the singular item or system.
Redundancy	Redundant systems can provide a more robust capacity.
Decentralization	Decentralization can introduce redundancy directly or disperse singularities, making them harder to target.
VV&A, Software/Hardware Engineering, Evaluations, Testing	Engineering, VV&A, evaluations, and testing can make singular components more robust.
Control of Exposure, Access, and Output	Control of exposure, access, and output can directly protect the singularity.
Hardening	Hardening can directly protect a singularity and make it more difficult to damage.
Fault, Uncertainty, Validity, and Quality Tolerance and Graceful Degradation	Singular components that can operate under faults and difficult conditions are less likely to fail.
Threat Response Structures and Plans	Many response plans introduce backups and contingencies that work around singularities.
Rapid Reconstitution and Recovery	Rapid recovery can reduce the effects of losing a singular component.
Adaptability and Learning	This provides learning or adaptation materials and plans to allow others to rapidly fill singularities.
Secondary	
Centralization	Centralized control can help manage access to and protect a singularity.
Trust Learning and Enforcement Systems	Trust systems can be particularly important for singular systems to help control access and exposure.
Non-Repudiation	Non-repudiation can be particularly important for singular systems to provide deterrence and evidence of untrustworthy behavior.
Static Resource Allocation	Static resource allocations can help to work around and prevent overtaxing singularities.
Dynamic Resource Allocation	Dynamic resource allocations can help to work around and prevent overtaxing singularities.
General Management	Proper management procedures, such as quality control, training, general security, and procedural control, can help to protect singularities.
Intelligence Operations	Intelligence can identify which singularities our adversaries know about.
Self-Awareness, Monitoring, and Assessments	Self-assessments can identify singularities.
General Counterintelligence	CI can prevent adversaries from knowing about vulnerable singularities.
Unpredictable to Adversary	CI can prevent adversaries from knowing about vulnerable singularities.
Deception for CI	Deceptions can hide singularities.
Denial of ISR and Target Acquisition	ISR denials can hide singularities.

Table A.2

Mitigation Techniques That Address Uniqueness

Primary	
Heterogeneity	Heterogeneity provides alternatives to the unique item or system.
Redundancy	Redundant systems (even if of the same unique type) can provide backups or parts during failure of a unique system.
VV&A, Software/Hardware Engineering, Evaluations, Testing	Engineering, VV&A, evaluations, and testing can make unique components more robust.
Control of Exposure, Access, and Output	Control of exposure, access, and output can directly protect the unique component.
Hardening	Hardening can directly protect a unique system and make it more difficult to damage.
Fault, Uncertainty, Validity, and Quality Tolerance and Graceful Degradation	Unique components that can operate under faults and difficult conditions are less likely to fail.
Threat Response Structures and Plans	Many response plans introduce backups and contingencies that provide new alternatives to unique items.
Rapid Reconstitution and Recovery	Rapid recovery can reduce the effects of losing a unique component.
Secondary	
Centralization	A unique item at a central location could be monitored, maintained, and repaired more effectively.
Decentralization	Decentralization can introduce redundancy directly or disperse unique systems, making them harder to target.
Static Resource Allocation	Static resource allocations can help to work around and prevent overtaxing unique systems.
Dynamic Resource Allocation	Dynamic resource allocations can help to work around and prevent overtaxing unique systems.
General Management	Proper management procedures, such as quality control, training, general security, and procedural control, can help to protect unique systems.
Intelligence Operations	Intelligence can identify which unique components our adversaries know about.
Self-Awareness, Monitoring, and Assessments	Self-assessments can identify uniqueness in our systems.
General CI	CI can prevent adversaries from knowing about unique, vulnerable components.
Unpredictable to Adversary	CI can prevent adversaries from knowing about unique, vulnerable components.
Deception for CI	Deceptions can hide the uniqueness of components.
Denial of ISR and Target Acquisition	ISR denials can hide the uniqueness of components.
Criminal and Legal Penalties and Guarantees	Warrantees and guarantees serve as useful ways to certify the capabilities and stability of unique items and can provide (often longer-term) remedies for failures.

Table A.3

Mitigation Techniques That Address or Are Facilitated by Centrality

Primary	
Decentralization	Decentralization directly addresses centrality concerns.
VV&A, Software/Hardware Engineering, Evaluations, Testing	Engineering, VV&A, evaluations, and testing can make centralized systems more robust.
Control of Exposure, Access, and Output	Control of exposure, access, and output can directly protect centralized components.
Hardening	Hardening can directly protect a centralized system and make it more difficult to damage.
Fault, Uncertainty, Validity, and Quality Tolerance and Graceful Degradation	Centralized systems that can operate under faults and difficult conditions are less likely to fail.
Threat Response Structures and Plans	Many response plans develop ways to protect and back up centralized capabilities.
Preventive and Retributive Information/Military Operations	Centralized facilities are often higher-value targets for adversaries, thus warranting a strong and aggressive response if damaged.
Secondary	
Heterogeneity	Heterogeneity reduces the variety of systems that would have to be compromised, even if they are still maintained at a central site.
Redundancy	Even if centralized, redundant systems can provide more-robust capability.
Trust Learning and Enforcement Systems	Trust systems can be particularly important for centralized systems to help control access and exposure.
Non-Repudiation	Non-repudiation can be particularly important for centralized systems to provide deterrence and evidence of untrustworthy behavior.
General Management	Proper management procedures, such as quality control, training, general security, and procedural control, can help to protect centralized systems.
Rapid Reconstitution and Recovery	Rapid recovery can reduce the effects of losing the centralized components and can in fact be facilitated by centrality.
Immunological Defense Systems	The ability of these systems to share information with decentralized nodes can mitigate the reason(s) for centrality.
Intelligence Operations	Intelligence can identify which singularities our adversaries know about.
Self-Awareness, Monitoring, and Assessments	Self-assessments can characterize the scope of our dependence on centralized systems.
General CI	CI can prevent adversaries from locating and characterizing our centralities.
Unpredictable to Adversary	CI can prevent adversaries from locating and characterizing our centralities.
Deception for CI	Deceptions can hide the centrality of a system.
Denial of ISR and Target Acquisition	ISR details can hide the centrality of a system.

Table A.3—Continued

Facilitated by Centrality	
Centralization	Leverage centrality to maximum advantage (e.g., quality control, consistency).
Adaptability and Learning	Centrality can facilitate learning and adaptation through improved self-awareness and feedback. Dissemination of lessons learned is also facilitated by centrality.
Deception for ISR	Centrality could enable and coordinate deception to improve ISR.
Law Enforcement; Civil Proceedings	Centralized items are often easier for law enforcement to protect.

Table A.4

Mitigation Techniques That Address or Are Facilitated by Homogeneity

Primary	
Heterogeneity	Heterogeneity is the opposite of homogeneity, introducing a range of different alternative systems.
VV&A, Software/Hardware Engineering, Evaluations, Testing	Engineering, VV&A, evaluations, and testing can be more extensive on homogeneous systems and make them more robust than heterogeneous systems.
Hardening	Hardening a homogeneous system can make it less vulnerable to attack.
Fault, Uncertainty, Validity, and Quality Tolerance and Graceful Degradation	Homogeneous systems that can operate under faults and difficult conditions are less likely to fail in general.
Secondary	
Redundancy	While not reducing the homogeneity, redundant items can make those systems more robust and able to withstand failures.
Decentralization	Dispersal of homogeneous targets makes them harder to attack all at once.
Control of Exposure, Access, and Output	Control of exposure, access, and output can directly protect homogeneous components. Homogeneous systems can facilitate control design.
General Management	Proper management procedures, such as quality control, training, general security, and procedural control, can help to protect homogeneous systems. Note that homogeneous systems can help facilitate management of information systems.
Self-Awareness, Monitoring, and Assessments	Self-assessments can determine how heterogeneous our systems have become.
General CI	CI can prevent adversaries from understanding what systems we have standardized on.
Unpredictable to Adversary	CI can prevent adversaries from understanding what systems we have standardized on.
Deception for CI	False heterogeneity can hide reliance on homogeneous components.
Denial of ISR and Target Acquisition	ISR denials can prevent adversaries from understanding what systems we have standardized on.
Facilitated by Homogeneity	
Static Resource Allocation	Note that homogeneous systems can facilitate resource allocations.
Dynamic Resource Allocation	Note that homogeneous systems can facilitate resource allocations.
General Management	Proper management procedures, such as quality control, training, general security, and procedural control, can help to protect homogeneous systems. Note that homogeneous systems can help facilitate management of information systems.

Table A.4—Continued

Rapid Reconstitution and Recovery	Homogeneity can facilitate reconstitution and recovery due to the availability of alternative systems and parts as well as common training and knowledge about those components.
Immunological Defense Systems	Homogeneity can make it easier to apply lessons learned from other nodes.
Vaccination	Homogeneity can make it easier to apply lessons learned from other nodes.

Table A.5

Mitigation Techniques That Address or Are Facilitated by Separability

Primary	
Centralization	Centralized systems will be harder to separate.
VV&A, Software/Hardware Engineering, Evaluations, Testing	Engineering, VV&A, evaluations, and testing can look for ways that system components can be isolated and develop ways to reduce this vulnerability.
Fault, Uncertainty, Validity, and Quality Tolerance and Graceful Degradation	Systems that can operate despite degraded conditions and uncertainty are harder to partition.
General Management	Proper management and coordination can help ensure cohesion and communication.
Self-Awareness, Monitoring, and Assessments	Monitoring can determine breaks in system interfaces, facilitating their restoration. Assessments can identify how separations have happened in the past, informing corrective measures.
Secondary	
Control of Exposure, Access, and Output	Control of exposure, access, and output can protect against separability.
Trust Learning and Enforcement Systems	Trust systems can inform interface controllers and reduce the likelihood of deceptive separations.
Hardening	Hardening system interfaces can make them more difficult to break.
Adaptability and Learning	Adaptation could help to learn and recognize attempts to partition the system.
Immunological Defense Systems	Information sharing can preclude the need to isolate systems under attack and share information about such attacks and how to defend against them.
Vaccination	Simulated attacks could uncover separability risks and force mitigation evaluations.
Intelligence Operations	Information about attacks can speed efforts to reconnect components and tune our own partitioning activities.
General CI	CI can reduce an adversary's understanding of how to separate system components.
Unpredictable to Adversary	CI can reduce an adversary's understanding of how to separate system components.
Deception for CI	Deceptions can make it harder to know how to separate system components.
Denial of ISR and Target Acquisition	ISR denials can reduce an adversary's understanding of how to separate system components.
Facilitated by Separability	
Deception for ISR	Known separabilities can be used in our deceptions to determine adversary's general knowledge, capabilities, and specific knowledge about us.

Table A.6

Mitigation Techniques That Address Logic or Implementation Errors, Fallibility

Primary	
Heterogeneity	A variety of systems can complement each other if the systems have different failure conditions.
VV&A, Software/Hardware Engineering, Evaluations, Testing	Engineering, VV&A, evaluations, and testing can identify errors and fallibilities while recommending solutions.
Control of Exposure, Access, and Output	Exposure, access, and output controls can be used to isolate the rest of the system from component errors and fallibilities.
Hardening	Hardening can remove errors and make it less fallible.
Fault, Uncertainty, Validity, and Quality Tolerance and Graceful Degradation	Tolerant systems are able to handle errors better when they happen.
General Management	Management reviews and quality control can help to recognize and avoid errors and fallibilities.
Adaptability and Learning	Examination of performance can help to locate errors and adjust to them.
Immunological Defense Systems	Some systems automatically recognize, update, patch, or correct errors.
Vaccination	Vaccination uncovers and repairs errors directly.
Secondary	
Centralization	Flawed systems will be easier to manage, control, and repair if they are at a central location.
Decentralization	It can be harder to understand and exploit the errors in systems when they are dispersed.
Trust Learning and Enforcement Systems	Trust learning can reduce fallibilities due to excessive accesses and reasoning about protections.
Static Resource Allocation	Resource allocations can work around errors and failures.
Dynamic Resource Allocation	Resource allocations can work around errors and failures.
Threat Response Structures and Plans	Many response plans introduce backups and contingencies that reduce fallibilities or minimize the effects of errors.
Rapid Reconstitution and Recovery	A rapid recovery capability reduces (but usually does not eliminate) the effect of component losses and errors.
Self-Awareness, Monitoring, and Assessments	Monitoring and assessments can look for errors and fallibilities.
General CI	CI can reduce an adversary's understanding of system errors and fallibilities.
Unpredictable to Adversary	CI can reduce an adversary's understanding of system errors and fallibilities.
Deception for CI	Deceptions can reduce an adversary's understanding of system errors and fallibilities.
Denial of ISR and Target Acquisition	ISR details can reduce an adversary's understanding of system errors and fallibilities.
Criminal and Legal Penalties and Guarantees	Warrantees and bonding can provide remediation for failed systems and motivate manufacturers to eliminate problems in the first place.
Law Enforcement; Civil Proceedings	Warrantees and bonding can provide remediation for failed systems.

Table A.7

Mitigation Techniques That Address or Are Facilitated by Design Sensitivity, Fragility, Limits, or Finiteness

Primary	
Heterogeneity	A variety of systems can complement each other if they have different sensitivities, fragilities, operating ranges, or limit dimensions.
Redundancy	Redundant systems can provide fallback capability or help spread the processing load if limits are reached.
Decentralization	It can be harder to understand and exploit the fragilities and limits in systems when they are dispersed. Decentralization can also introduce improved capacity that might be exploited if information processing can be partitioned. Dispersed systems can also be used as alternative capacity when local limits are reached.
VV&A, Software/Hardware Engineering, Evaluations, Testing	Engineering, VV&A, evaluations, and testing can identify and resolve sensitivities, fragilities, and limits.
Control of Exposure, Access, and Output	Controls can help to protect fragile systems from harsh environments or overloading attacks.
Hardening	Hardening can make the design less fragile.
Fault, Uncertainty, Validity, and Quality Tolerance and Graceful Degradation	Tolerant systems are able to handle fragilities, sensitivities, and limits better when they happen.
Static Resource Allocation	Resource allocations can balance loads to prevent failures and partition work to avoid sensitivities.
Dynamic Resource Allocation	Resource allocations can balance loads to prevent failures and partition work to avoid sensitivities.
General Management	Attentive management can avoid overloading systems and stressing fragile components.
Self-Awareness, Monitoring, and Assessments	Status monitoring can help management prevent the system from crossing limits, avoid sensitivities, etc. Assessments can continue to identify unknown fragilities and limits.
Secondary	
Centralization	Fragile and limited systems will be easier to control their loads and inputs if centralized.
Threat Response Structures and Plans	Response plans can provide additional resources to minimize limits and the effects of design sensitivities if they are known.
Rapid Reconstitution and Recovery	A rapid recovery capability reduces (but usually does not eliminate) the effect of component losses due to fragility and crossing limitations.
Adaptability and Learning	Examination of performance can help to locate fragilities and limits while developing work-arounds.
Immunological Defense Systems	Some systems automatically alert, fuse, recognize, update, patch, and correct sensitivities.
Vaccination	Vaccination uncovers fragilities and limits directly. Some may be corrected directly, while others could be avoided in the future.
Intelligence Operations	Information on attacks that target limitations and sensitivities can be used to plan and implement countermeasures.
Attack Detection, Recognition, Damage Assessment, and Forensics (Self and Foe)	Behavior and condition monitoring can help to characterize sensitivities, limits, and fragilities.
General CI	CI can reduce an adversary's understanding of system sensitivities and limits.
Unpredictable to Adversary	CI can reduce an adversary's understanding of system sensitivities and limits.

Table A.7—Continued

Deception for CI	Deceptions can reduce an adversary's understanding of system sensitivities and limits.
Denial of ISR and Target Acquisition	ISR denials can reduce an adversary's understanding of system sensitivities and limits.
Criminal and Legal Penalties and Guarantees	Warrantees and bonding can provide remediation for failed systems and motivate manufacturers to eliminate problems in the first place.
Law Enforcement; Civil Proceedings	Warrantees and bonding can provide remediation for failed systems.
Facilitated by Design Sensitivity, Fragility, Limits, or Finiteness	
Deception for ISR	Known sensitivities can be used in our deceptions to determine adversary's general knowledge, capabilities, and specific knowledge about us.

Table A.8

Mitigation Techniques That Address Unrecoverability

Primary	
Heterogeneity	Different systems may fail at different times, helping to avoid a complete system failure.
Redundancy	Redundant systems can provide fallback capability in the event of an unrecoverable failure.
Decentralization	Decentralized operations can provide alternative capacity if parts of the system fail.
VV&A, Software/Hardware Engineering, Evaluations, Testing	Engineering, VV&A, evaluations, and testing can help to identify why a system is unrecoverable and can recommend remedies.
Hardening	Hardening can make the system less likely to fail in the first place.
Fault, Uncertainty, Validity, and Quality Tolerance and Graceful Degradation	Tolerant systems are less likely to fail in the first place.
Rapid Reconstitution and Recovery	Rapid reconstitution and recovery directly addresses unrecoverability.
Self-Awareness, Monitoring, and Assessments	Early detection of unrecoverable failures can speed the implementation of recovery procedures, inform how to avoid failures in the future, and inform ways to make the systems more recoverable in the first place.
Secondary	
Centralization	Unrecoverable systems will be easier to protect from failure in the first place if they are in a central location close to management.
Control of Exposure, Access, and Output	Partitions and isolations can help to limit the scope of damage from an unrecoverable component.
Static Resource Allocation	Resource allocations can sometimes work around unrecoverable failures.
Dynamic Resource Allocation	Resource allocations can sometimes work around unrecoverable failures.
General Management	Management can help avoid failure in the first place.
Threat Response Structures and Plans	Response plans can provide backups and contingencies in the event of unrecoverable failures.
Adaptability and Learning	Learning can help to avoid unrecoverable conditions in the future.
Immunological Defense Systems	Unrecoverability may be preempted on other systems once an attack is recognized and understood.
Vaccination	Attacks can highlight unrecoverabilities and might introduce mitigation ideas.

Table A.8—Continued

Intelligence Operations	ISR can inform us of attacks and prompt us to protect unrecoverable assets. It can also inform us of specific attacks and help filter them.
Attack Detection, Recognition, Damage Assessment, and Forensics (Self and Foe)	Better analysis of failures can help to understand what caused the failure, avoid failure conditions in the future, and correct failure modes in the first place.
General CI	CI can reduce an adversary's understanding of what components are unrecoverable.
Unpredictable to Adversary	CI can reduce an adversary's understanding of what components are unrecoverable.
Deception for CI	Deceptions can reduce an adversary's understanding of what components are unrecoverable.
Denial of ISR and Target Acquisition	ISR denials can reduce an adversary's understanding of what components are unrecoverable.
Criminal and Legal Penalties and Guarantees	Warrantees and bonding can provide remediation for failed systems and motivate manufacturers to eliminate problems in the first place.
Law Enforcement; Civil Proceedings	Warrantees and bonding can provide remediation for failed systems.

Table A.9

Mitigation Techniques That Address Behavioral Sensitivity or Fragility

Primary	
Heterogeneity	Heterogeneous systems with different sensitivities and fragilities can provide alternative capabilities.
Redundancy	Redundant systems can help to compensate for behavioral sensitivities and fragilities.
Decentralization	It can be harder to understand and exploit the fragilities and limits in systems when they are dispersed. Also, dispersed systems of autonomous, heterogeneous entities can provide more-robust behavior.
VV&A, Software/Hardware Engineering, Evaluations, Testing	Engineering, VV&A, evaluations, and testing can identify and resolve behavioral sensitivities and fragilities.
Control of Exposure, Access, and Output	Controls can help to protect fragile systems from harsh environments or overloading attacks.
Hardening	Hardening can make the behavior less fragile and sensitive.
Fault, Uncertainty, Validity, and Quality Tolerance and Graceful Degradation	Tolerant systems are able to handle fragilities, sensitivities, and limits better when they happen.
Static Resource Allocation	Resource allocations can balance loads to prevent failures and partition work to avoid sensitivities.
Dynamic Resource Allocation	Resource allocations can balance loads to prevent failures and partition work to avoid sensitivities.
General Management	Attentive management can avoid stressing fragile components and control behavioral sensitivities.
Self-Awareness, Monitoring, and Assessments	Status monitoring can help management prevent the system from crossing entering sensitive operating conditions. Assessments can continue to identify unknown fragilities and sensitivities.
Secondary	
Centralization	Behavioral sensitivities and fragilities are easier to observe and manage if they are centralized.

Table A.9—Continued

Threat Response Structures and Plans	Response plans can provide additional resources to minimize limits and the effects of design sensitivities.
Rapid Reconstitution and Recovery	A rapid recovery capability reduces (but usually does not eliminate) the effect of component losses due to fragility and crossing limitations.
Adaptability and Learning	Examination of performance can help to locate fragilities and limits while developing work-arounds.
Immunological Defense Systems	Some systems automatically alert, fuse, recognize, update, patch, and correct sensitivities.
Vaccination	Vaccination uncovers fragilities and limits directly. Some may be corrected directly, while others could be avoided in the future.
Intelligence Operations	Information on attacks that target sensitivities and fragilities can be used to plan and implement countermeasures.
Attack Detection, Recognition, Damage Assessment, and Forensics (Self and Foe)	Behavior and condition monitoring can help to characterize sensitivities, limits, and fragilities.
General CI	CI can reduce an adversary's understanding of system sensitivities and fragilities.
Unpredictable to Adversary	CI can reduce an adversary's understanding of system sensitivities and fragilities.
Deception for CI	Deceptions can reduce an adversary's understanding of system sensitivities and fragilities.
Denial of ISR and Target Acquisition	ISR details can reduce an adversary's understanding of system sensitivities and fragilities.
Criminal and Legal Penalties and Guarantees	Warrantees and bonding can provide remediation for failed systems and motivate manufacturers to eliminate problems in the first place.
Law Enforcement; Civil Proceedings	Warrantees and bonding can provide remediation for failed systems.

Table A.10

Mitigation Techniques That Address Malevolence

Primary	
VV&A, Software/Hardware Engineering, Evaluations, Testing	Engineering, VV&A, evaluations, and testing can identify and resolve malevolent tendencies.
Control of Exposure, Access, and Output	Controls can help to keep out or wrap malevolent components, isolating critical systems, and performing deeper checks for malevolence in critical areas.
Trust Learning and Enforcement Systems	Trust learning and enforcement systems can help to identify and control malevolent behavior and entities.
Non-Repudiation	Non-repudiation can add source information to malevolent behaviors and provide deterrence to malevolent entities.
General Management	Management can actively monitor for malevolent actors.
Intelligence Operations	Intelligence can specifically look for malevolent actors.
Self-Awareness, Monitoring, and Assessments	Monitoring can identify malevolent actors early on.
Deception for ISR	Deceptions can be valuable ways to draw out malevolent actors.

Table A.10—Continued

Attack Detection, Recognition, Damage Assessment, and Forensics (Self and Foe)	Monitoring and assessments directly look for malevolent actors.
General CI	CI looks for malevolent insiders that are supplying intelligence on the system.
Unpredictable to Adversary	CI looks for malevolent insiders that are supplying intelligence on the system.
Deception for CI	Deceptions can identify malevolent insiders supplying intelligence on the system.
Denial of ISR and Target Acquisition	ISR detail can help prevent malevolent actors from knowing where to strike.
Deterrence	Deterrence can dampen malevolent tendencies.
Preventive and Retributive Information/Military Operations	Active operations can eliminate or contain malevolent actors.
Criminal and Legal Penalties and Guarantees	Penalties can deter malevolent actors or actively restrain them if caught.
Law Enforcement; Civil Proceedings	Enforcement can restrain malevolent actors.
Secondary	
Heterogeneity	Different systems may have different malevolent tendencies, weaknesses, or even lack malevolence altogether, mitigating the risks from the malevolent system.
Redundancy	Redundancy could reduce the effectiveness of a single system gone bad.
Decentralization	Malevolent entities are less effective when control and processing is dispersed, since it requires more effort and purview over a wider range of dispersed systems.
Threat Response Structures and Plans	Well-developed plans can reduce the access of and damage done by malevolent actors.
Immunological Defense Systems	Monitoring and sharing will reduce the ability of malevolent entities to remain hidden or to jump to new systems and remain undetected.
Vaccination	Simulated attacks can sensitize the system to malevolence.

Table A.11

Mitigation Techniques That Address Rigidity

Primary	
VV&A, Software/Hardware Engineering, Evaluations, Testing	Engineering, VV&A, evaluations, and testing can identify rigidities and recommend remedies.
Trust Learning and Enforcement Systems	Trust systems adapt system accesses and information use to changing behaviors and new entities.
Fault, Uncertainty, Validity, and Quality Tolerance and Graceful Degradation	Tolerant systems are more accepting and can operate in broader ranges of inputs.
Dynamic Resource Allocation	Dynamic allocations should adjust to current conditions.
General Management	Active management can react to new problems and pursue solutions.
Threat Response Structures and Plans	Plans can be adaptive to the current situation, especially when they provide general context, arrangements, and alternatives in which local responders can work.

Table A.11—Continued

Rapid Reconstitution and Recovery	Rapid reconstitution and recovery can provide flexibility through failure responsiveness.
Adaptability and Learning	Dynamic adaptation and learning can adjust system configurations to match current needs.
Immunological Defense Systems	These systems look for new threats and solutions. When found, they share information and provide rapid updates and changes to the system.
Vaccination	Vaccination shows where the system needs to be changed.
Secondary	
Heterogeneity	Different systems may be rigid in different ways. Their differences may highlight rigidities in the original system.
Decentralization	Decentralized systems tend to be more innovative, flexible, and adaptive to local conditions.
Static Resource Allocation	Static allocations can introduce some level of response to current conditions.
Self-Awareness, Monitoring, and Assessments	Monitoring and assessments can identify rigidities.
Attack Detection, Recognition, Damage Assessment, and Forensics (Self and Foe)	Understanding attacks often lead to internal changes to improve security.
General CI	CI can reduce an adversary's understanding of the system's rigidities.
Unpredictable to Adversary	CI can reduce an adversary's understanding of the system's rigidities.
Deception for CI	Deceptions can reduce an adversary's understanding of the system's rigidities.
Denial of ISR and Target Acquisition	ISR denial can reduce an adversary's understanding of the system's rigidities.

Table A.12

Mitigation Techniques That Address Malleability

Primary	
VV&A, Software/Hardware Engineering, Evaluations, Testing	Engineering, VV&A, evaluations, and testing can identify where the system is malleable and can recommend remedies.
Trust Learning and Enforcement Systems	Trust systems introduce more rigor and oversight to make it harder to control and manipulate the information system.
Hardening	Hardening can make the system less changeable and less modifiable.
General Management	Management oversight can monitor for undesirable changes and manipulations.
Threat Response Structures and Plans	Plans provide structure to the operation and contingency, reducing the likelihood that the system can be manipulated.
Self-Awareness, Monitoring, and Assessments	Systems are harder to manipulate if they are self-aware and can see if you are trying to manipulate them.
Deterrence	Deterrence can sensitize actors and make them less controllable.
Secondary	
Heterogeneity	Different systems may have different maleabilities.
Centralization	Centralized systems can be more effectively controlled and thus less prone to manipulation.

Table A.12—Continued

Decentralization	It is harder to change an entire distributed system than a centralized, monolithic one.
Control of Exposure, Access, and Output	Controls make it less likely that a system can be changed without proper authorization.
Non-Repudiation	Systems can be less likely to be manipulated if source information is always provided.
Static Resource Allocation	Preplanned allocations can prevent manipulation of allocation configurations.
Adaptability and Learning	The system will be less likely to be manipulated if it actively examines performance and adjusts to new situations.
Attack Detection, Recognition, Damage Assessment, and Forensics (Self and Foe)	Understanding and knowledge of attacks can make entities less controllable and can identify unprotected control points for future remediation.
General CI	CI can reduce an adversary's understanding of the system's control points and manipulabilities.
Unpredictable to Adversary	CI can reduce an adversary's understanding of the system's control points and manipulabilities.
Deception for CI	Deceptions can reduce an adversary's understanding of the system's control points and manipulabilities.
Denial of ISR and Target Acquisition	ISR denial can reduce an adversary's understanding of the system's control points and manipulabilities.
Criminal and Legal Penalties and Guarantees	The existence of penalties can make deterrence more effective.

Table A.13

Mitigation Techniques that Address Gullibility, Deceivability, or Naiveté

Primary	
VV&A, Software/Hardware Engineering, Evaluations, Testing	Engineering, VV&A, evaluations, and testing can examine system gullibility and recommend compensations.
Trust Learning and Enforcement Systems	Trust systems introduce more rigor and oversight to make it harder to fool the information system.
Hardening	Hardening can make the system more knowledgeable and insistent on reliable information sources.
General Management	Management oversight can monitor for undesirable changes, share threat knowledge, and provide advice.
Threat Response Structures and Plans	Plans provide structure to the operation and contingency, reducing the likelihood that the system can be blindly manipulated.
Adaptability and Learning	Attention and adaptation to the current situation can reduce blind behavior.
Vaccination	Simulated attacks can sensitize the system and make it less gullible.
Intelligence Operations	Intelligence can provide information about our adversaries and their techniques.
Self-Awareness, Monitoring, and Assessments	Systems are harder to manipulate if they are self-aware and can see if you are trying to manipulate them.
Secondary	
Control of Exposure, Access, and Output	Controls are often implemented with significant forethought and can avoid some naive conditions.
Non-Repudiation	It can be harder to deceive a system if source information is provided.

Table A.13—Continued

Static Resource Allocation	Static allocations often are well engineered in advance.
Immunological Defense Systems	The adaptive, sharing, and automatic maintenance nature of these systems makes it harder to attack parts of the system based on noncompliance or ignorance of the latest information.
Attack Detection, Recognition, Damage Assessment, and Forensics (Self and Foe)	Understanding and knowledge of attacks can make entities less gullible and less naive to the same ruses.
General CI	CI can reduce an adversary's understanding of system biases and operations, making it more difficult to manipulate it.
Unpredictable to Adversary	CI can reduce an adversary's understanding of system biases and operations, making it more difficult to manipulate it.
Deception for CI	Deceptions can reduce an adversary's understanding of system biases and operations, making it more difficult to manipulate it.
Denial of ISR and Target Acquisition	ISR denial can reduce an adversary's understanding of system biases and operations, making it more difficult to manipulate it.

Table A.14

Mitigation Techniques That Address Complacency

Primary	
VV&A, Software/Hardware Engineering, Evaluations, Testing	Engineering, VV&A, evaluations, and testing can help to keep systems from being complacent by identifying weaknesses and ensuring proper procedures.
Trust Learning and Enforcement Systems	Trust systems adapt system accesses and information use to changing behaviors and new entities.
Dynamic Resource Allocation	Dynamic attention to resource allocation draws attention to current conditions.
General Management	Active management can continue to look for and adapt to new threats.
Threat Response Structures and Plans	Planning engages people in active consideration of vulnerabilities and sets up contingency systems to facilitate response.
Adaptability and Learning	Attention and adaptation to the current situation and system performance directly reduce complacency.
Immunological Defense Systems	These systems are always on the alert for suspicious activity and problems.
Intelligence Operations	Current and detailed understanding of adversary activities can motivate us out of complacency.
Self-Awareness, Monitoring, and Assessments	Direct knowledge of internal activities and attacks can motivate people to action.
Deterrence	Warnings and penalties can deter actors from becoming complacent.
Secondary	
Centralization	Centralization can introduce regularly scheduled security reviews and procedures, thus reducing complacency.
Control of Exposure, Access, and Output	Additional attention to controls can reduce complacency if they are actively maintained and improved.
Vaccination	Simulated attacks can sensitize the system and keep it alert.
Attack Detection, Recognition, Damage Assessment, and Forensics (Self and Foe)	Knowledge of the real dangers based on prior attacks will make entities less complacent. Automated analysis systems can be tied to protective systems and directly reduce complacency.

Table A.14—Continued

General CI	Knowledge about intelligence risks can motivate people to pay better attention to security.
Unpredictable to Adversary	Knowledge about intelligence risks can motivate people to pay better attention to security.
Deception for CI	Knowledge about intelligence risks can motivate people to pay better attention to security.
Criminal and Legal Penalties and Guarantees	Penalties can make warnings and deterrence more intimidating.

Table A.15

Mitigation Techniques That Address Corruptibility or Controllability

Primary	
VV&A, Software/Hardware Engineering, Evaluations, Testing	Engineering, VV&A, evaluations, and testing can identify and remedy weaknesses that can be exploited.
Control of Exposure, Access, and Output	Control filters can protect against common control problems and vulnerabilities.
Trust Learning and Enforcement Systems	Trust systems introduce more rigor and oversight to make it harder to control and manipulate the information system.
Hardening	Hardening can make the system more knowledgeable and insistent on reliable information sources.
General Management	Management oversight can monitor for undesirable changes and manipulations.
Immunological Defense Systems	Use of the latest and best security knowledge and procedures will make it harder to directly attack the system.
Intelligence Operations	Intelligence can monitor for corruption directly and identify adversary capabilities and activities that indicate control and access to your system.
Self-Awareness, Monitoring, and Assessments	Self-monitoring can identify corruption. Assessments can identify controllability points and corruptibility danger signs (e.g., personal problems, careless behavior).
Deterrence	Deterrence can reduce corruptibility and controllability of actors.
Secondary	
Heterogeneity	Different systems may have different corruptible or controllable weaknesses or have such weaknesses in different areas so they can help compensate for the other's weaknesses.
Centralization	Centralized control can help to monitor and deal with corruption and usurped control.
Decentralization	It is harder to corrupt or control an entire distributed system than a centralized, monolithic one.
Non-Repudiation	Some repudiation systems protect information content from corruption or confirm the source of system updates.
Vaccination	Simulated attacks can sensitize the system and keep it alert to corruptions.
Attack Detection, Recognition, Damage Assessment, and Forensics (Self and Foe)	Understanding and knowledge of attacks can make entities less controllable and can identify unprotected control points for future remediation.
General CI	Assessments can identify controllability points and corruptibility danger signs (e.g., personal problems, careless behavior).

Table A.15—Continued

Unpredictable to Adversary	Assessments can identify controllability points and corruptibility danger signs (e.g., personal problems, careless behavior).
Deception for CI	Deceptions can reduce an adversary's understanding of the system's control points and corruptibility.
Criminal and Legal Penalties and Guarantees	Penalties can make warnings and deterrence more intimidating.

Table A.16

Mitigation Techniques That Address Accessible, Detectable, Identifiable, Transparent, or Interceptable

Primary	
Decentralization	Decentralized systems are harder to detect, identify, track, access, and intercept in their entirety.
VV&A, Software/Hardware Engineering, Evaluations, Testing	Engineering, VV&A, evaluations, and testing can examine and remedy weaknesses that can be exploited.
Control of Exposure, Access, and Output	These controls are directly designed to reduce accessibilities, detectabilities, and interceptions.
Trust Learning and Enforcement Systems	Trust systems can adapt system restrict accesses and exposures to reliable entities.
Hardening	Hardening can make the system less accessible, less interceptable, and less likely to be damaged if access is compromised.
Fault, Uncertainty, Validity, and Quality Tolerance and Graceful Degradation	Tolerant systems can be less likely to be compromised or damaged if access is compromised.
Threat Response Structures and Plans	Response plans can reduce visibility and exposure based on (perceived) threats and conditions.
General CI	CI works directly to minimize adversarial capability to detect, identify, access, and intercept system components.
Unpredictable to Adversary	CI works directly to minimize adversarial capability to detect, identify, access, and intercept system components.
Deception for CI	Deceptions can directly mask detections, identifications, and transparencies.
Denial of ISR and Target Acquisition	Denials can directly mask detections, identifications, and transparencies.
Deterrence	Deterrence can increase the cost of monitoring and interception while making them more evident.
Preventive and Retributive Information/Military Operations	Active retributions can protect access points, increase the cost of monitoring and interception, and make compromises more evident.
Secondary	
Heterogeneity	A range of different system types would be harder to track, identify, and access.
Redundancy	Multiple systems can be harder to identify and track.
General Management	Active and well-planned management can help to minimize exposures and interceptions.
Immunological Defense Systems	Vigilance and automatic sharing can keep exposure controls at their peak.
Vaccination	Attacks on exposure controls can strengthen our understanding of their weaknesses, identify misconfigurations, and motivate action.

Table A.16—Continued

Intelligence Operations	Intelligence about adversary's sensor capabilities can inform our countermeasure designs and operating procedures.
Self-Awareness, Monitoring, and Assessments	The more we understand our own systems and their exposure, the better we can design countermeasures to protect them.
Attack Detection, Recognition, Damage Assessment, and Forensics (Self and Foe)	Detection and forensics can identify weak points while possibly informing attack interception mechanisms in a current attack.
Criminal and Legal Penalties and Guarantees	Penalties can make warnings and deterrence more intimidating.
Law Enforcement; Civil Proceedings	Enforcement can provide physical protection at access points.

Table A.17

Mitigation Techniques That Address Hard to Manage or Control

Primary	
Centralization	Centralization can make it easier to manage and control operations.
VV&A, Software/Hardware Engineering, Evaluations, Testing	Engineering, VV&A, evaluations, and testing can examine why the system is hard to manage and control while making recommendations on how to improve these functions.
Control of Exposure, Access, and Output	Exposure, access, and output control structures can help in the management and control of the information flow into, out of, and within the information system.
Trust Learning and Enforcement Systems	Trust systems can introduce more rigor and support to management of the system, especially in environments containing entities of unknown reliability.
Static Resource Allocation	Resource allocation schemes introduce additional management control structures.
Dynamic Resource Allocation	Resource allocation schemes introduce additional management control structures.
General Management	Additional attention to management structures and control points can help to bring systems under control.
Threat Response Structures and Plans	Plans and contingencies provide additional ways to manage and control the system.
Self-Awareness, Monitoring, and Assessments	Self-information is a key prerequisite to effective management and control.
Secondary	
Immunological Defense Systems	The automatic nature of the system facilitates management, especially of distributed and diverse systems.
Attack Detection, Recognition, Damage Assessment, and Forensics (Self and Foe)	Improved understanding of operations and weaknesses can improve manageability.
Deterrence	Deterrence is a management tool to help control actors' behavior.
Criminal and Legal Penalties and Guarantees	Penalties can strengthen management's actions and warnings.
Law Enforcement; Civil Proceedings	Enforcement shows that disregard for management's actions will result in real penalties.

Table A.18

Mitigation Techniques That Address Self-Unawareness or Unpredictability

Primary	
Centralization	Centralization can make it easier to monitor and understand operations.
VV&A, Software/Hardware Engineering, Evaluations, Testing	Engineering, VV&A, evaluations, and testing can identify and resolve limits in self-awareness and unpredictability.
Trust Learning and Enforcement Systems	Trust systems add monitors to be more aware of what is happening in the system and attributing actions to entities.
Immunological Defense Systems	The self-monitoring component of these systems helps to provide insight into systemwide status and behavior.
Vaccination	Simulated attacks will provide additional information and insights into the information system and its operation under stress.
Self-Awareness, Monitoring, and Assessments	New techniques to gather information about our own system can directly address these deficiencies.
Attack Detection, Recognition, Damage Assessment, and Forensics (Self and Foe)	Monitoring and analysis will improve knowledge and awareness of the information system.
Secondary	
Static Resource Allocation	Resource allocations provide state information about the information system and its processing.
Dynamic Resource Allocation	Resource allocations provide state information about the information system and its processing.
General Management	Self-knowledge is an important step in setting up management structures and controls.
Threat Response Structures and Plans	Plans often introduce new sources of information about one's own system and control structures to reduce unpredictability.
General CI	CI often requires a sound understanding of our system as an intelligence target.
Unpredictable to Adversary	CI often requires a sound understanding of our system as an intelligence target.
Deception for CI	Deceptions often require a sound understanding of our system as an intelligence target.

Table A.19

Mitigation Techniques That Address or Are Facilitated by Predictability

Primary	
Heterogeneity	A range of different system types will require more resources to understand and predict how they will operate, especially if their interactions yield emergent behaviors.
VV&A, Software/Hardware Engineering, Evaluations, Testing	Engineering, VV&A, evaluations, and testing can identify and resolve excessive predictabilities in the system.
Dynamic Resource Allocation	Dynamic allocations can be less predictable, since they rely on current conditions.
Adaptability and Learning	Adaptation provides a moving target for the adversary to understand.
Immunological Defense Systems	The ability to rapidly insert modifications across the system can make it harder for an adversary to maintain a common operating picture of the information system and its configuration.

Table A.19—Continued

General CI	A major goal of counterintelligence is to reduce our adversary's ability to predict how our system works.
Unpredictable to Adversary	A major goal of counterintelligence is to reduce our adversary's ability to predict how our system works.
Deception for CI	Deceptions can make the information system harder to understand and predict.
Denial of ISR and Target Acquisition	Denial of enemy ISR interferes with the enemy's ability to predict the information system's structure and function.
Secondary	
Decentralization	Decentralized systems often contain a degree of autonomy and heterogeneity, making them less predictable.
Control of Exposure, Access, and Output	Controls can make it harder for adversaries to predict how the system is configured inside the protected areas.
General Management	Active and well-planned management can help to minimize dissemination of information about the information system.
Threat Response Structures and Plans	Plans can introduce adaptive alternatives and resources that make the system less predictable.
Vaccination	Repeated red teaming can keep the system in continual maintenance and make it less predictable.
Attack Detection, Recognition, Damage Assessment, and Forensics (Self and Foe)	Detection and forensics can identify predictable weak points that require corrective attention.
Facilitated by Predictability	
Deception for ISR	Predictabilities can be leveraged to dupe the attacker or prober to see how they behave and how much they know.

VULNERABILITIES THAT CAN BE INCURRED BY SECURITY TECHNIQUES

No vulnerability cautions have been identified for the following security techniques:

- Denial of ISR and Target Acquisition
- Preventive and Retributive Information/Military Operations

Table A.20

Vulnerabilities That Can Be Incurred from Heterogeneity

Primary Cautions	
Hard to Manage or Control	A variety of different system types can be difficult to manage, maintain, and interoperate.
Self-Unawareness and Unpredictability	A variety of different system types can be difficult to monitor and predict how they are interacting and operating.
Secondary Cautions	
Design Sensitivity/Fragility/Limits/Finiteness	A collection of heterogeneous systems may introduce design fragilities or lowest-common-denominator limits.
Behavioral Sensitivity/Fragility	A collection of heterogeneous systems may introduce behavioral sensitivities or fragilities due to their operating differences or management challenges.

Table A.21

Vulnerabilities That Can Be Incurred from Redundancy

Secondary Cautions	
Separability	Redundant systems (especially if located in different places) might be isolated and attacked separately.
Behavioral Sensitivity/Fragility	Redundant, heterogeneous systems could introduce voting paradoxes where the "best" decision may not be reached (e.g., decisions by committee are often weak compromises).
Hard to Manage or Control	Redundant systems could be harder to manage if proper procedures are not in place to control their interactions and to force proper decisions.

Table A.22

Vulnerabilities That Can Be Incurred from Centralization

Primary Cautions	
Centrality	Centralization introduces centrality directly by definition and must be judiciously implemented.
Rigidity	Centralized systems can become more stated and rigid, since they tend to reduce creative exploration and the use of alternative approaches.
Accessible/Detectable/Identifiable/Transparent/Interceptable	Centralization can make it easier for adversaries to locate, detect, and identify operations.

Table A.22—Continued

Secondary Cautions	
Singularity	Centralization could introduce singularities in the name of cost savings.
Homogeneity	Centralization efforts may have a tendency to homogenize the systems to simplify management and save money.
Complacency	Some centralized systems become complacent, since they are believed to be more robust.
Corruptibility/ Controllability	Centralized systems have control logic and paths that may be usurped.
Predictability	Centralized operations tend to be more stated, predefined, predictable, and less innovative.

Table A.23

Vulnerabilities That Can Be Incurred from Decentralization

Primary Cautions	
Separability	Dispersed items are easier to isolate and attack separately.
Hard to Manage or Control	Dispersed, decentralized systems can be harder to manage and control, since they require an extensive C4I coordination system.
Self-Unawareness and Unpredictability	It is harder to understand and track the operations of a decentralized system.
Secondary Cautions	
Logic/Implementation Errors; Fallibility	The logic and interoperability components in a decentralized system can make the system more complex and more prone to errors.
Design Sensitivity/ Fragility/Limits/ Finiteness	The logic and interoperability components in a decentralized system can make the system more complex and more prone to sensitivities and limits due to synchrony, coordination, and communication limitations.
Behavioral Sensitivity/Fragility	Decentralized systems (especially as they become more complex) can have behavioral anomalies.
Malleability	Decentralized, innovative nodes with less-centralized and -structured control might have less-rigorous testing and thus be more malleable.
Gullibility/Deceivability/ Naiveté	Decentralized, innovative nodes with less-centralized and -structured control might have less-rigorous management and thus be more gullible.

Table A.24

Vulnerabilities That Can Be Incurred from VV&A, Software/Hardware Engineering, Evaluations, Testing

Secondary Cautions	
Complacency	The existence of engineering, VV&A, evaluations, and testing can make a system's users and managers feel that it has already accounted for critical vulnerabilities and hence will become complacent, especially to novel threats.
Predictability	The use of standard engineering, VV&A, evaluations, and testing (and their reports and documentations) can introduce predictabilities in the system operations.

Table A.25

Vulnerabilities That Can Be Incurred from Control of Exposure, Access, and Output

Primary Cautions	
Separability	These controls often introduce separations and could be exploited to separate parts of an otherwise functioning system. Such separations can degrade overall performance while improving security.
Rigidity	Controls can make the system more rigid in general and harder to modify quickly.
Secondary Cautions	
Centrality	Controls are often centralized and may introduce another point of vulnerability.
Design Sensitivity/ Fragility/Limits/ Finiteness	Controls can introduce limits and sensitivities, since their filters are often imperfect and can interfere with legitimate communication.
Unrecoverability	Restricted communications can make it harder to monitor and quickly access systems for recovery purposes.
Behavioral Sensitivity/Fragility	Controls can introduce limits and sensitivities, since their filters are often imperfect and can interfere with legitimate communication.
Gullibility/Deceivability/ Naiveté	Any control relies on the use of a bias function to filter the interface; if understood, this bias can be exploited to deceive the control.
Complacency	Systems with extensive control are often thought of as secure and can become complacent to their imperfections.
Corruptibility/ Controllability	Extra control structures always introduce another point of potential controllability and corruption.
Hard to Manage or Control	Sophisticated control structures can be difficult to manage and control, requiring extensive training, experience, and knowledge.
Self-Unawareness and Unpredictability	Restricted accesses and controls can make it harder to monitor internal system conditions and predict how the system will perform.
Predictability	Some control systems are standard in the industry, with predictable limitations and default configurations.

Table A.26

Vulnerabilities That Can Be Incurred from Trust Learning and Enforcement Systems

Secondary Cautions	
Separability	Some trust models can be manipulated by introducing false information that separates trustworthy entities.
Malleability	Some trust models can be manipulated by introducing false information in order to establish trust.
Gullibility/Deceivability/ Naiveté	Models that gauge trusted behavior might be fooled if the bias function is known to an adversary.
Complacency	The use of a trust system can cause complacency if its limitations are not recognized and incorporated into vulnerability assessments.

Table A.27

Vulnerabilities That Can Be Incurred from Non-Repudiation

Secondary Caution	
Complacency	Rigorous non-repudiation can seem to provide significant security protections, but the information must be acted upon for it to be of maximal value.

Table A.28

Vulnerabilities That Can Be Incurred from Hardening

Primary Caution	
Rigidity	Hardening could make the system more rigid.
Secondary Cautions	
Design Sensitivity/ Fragility/Limits/ Finiteness	Sometimes hardening is at the expense of capacity.
Complacency	Hardened systems might be thought of as invulnerable.
Hard to Manage or Control	Rigid, hardened systems can be hard to manage or control, especially to changing conditions.
Self-Unawareness and Unpredictability	Some hardening approaches can make it harder to monitor and understand what is going on in the system and how it will react.
Predictability	Rigid, hardened systems can be more predictable to a knowledgeable adversary.

Table A.29

Vulnerabilities That Can Be Incurred from Fault, Uncertainty, Validity, and Quality Tolerance and Graceful Degradation

Secondary Cautions	
Design Sensitivity/ Fragility/Limits/ Finiteness	Sometimes systems with graceful degradation operate in a degraded fashion under conditions where other systems would operate flawlessly.
Complacency	Tolerant systems might be thought of as invulnerable.
Self-Unawareness and Unpredictability	Some tolerant and gracefully degrading approaches are hard for humans to understand how they work.

Table A.30

Vulnerabilities That Can Be Incurred from Static Resource Allocation

Primary Cautions	
Separability	Resource allocations can be exploited to attack or overwhelm partitions allocated to particular problems.
Rigidity	Static allocations might become inappropriate for the current situation.
Gullibility/Deceivability/ Naiveté	Adversaries could manipulate the system into less-desirable configurations. Static allocations may be inappropriate for current conditions.
Predictability	Static allocation plans introduce predictabilities if they are known.

Table A.30—Continued

Secondary Cautions	
Centrality	Static resource allocations may require centralized monitoring and control.
Malleability	Dynamic allocation triggers could be manipulated with activity to move the system into less-desirable configurations.
Complacency	The existence of allocation plans may make one feel overly secure.

Table A.31

Vulnerabilities That Can Be Incurred from Dynamic Resource Allocation

Secondary Cautions	
Centrality	Dynamic resource allocations may require centralized monitoring and control.
Separability	Some allocation approaches may be exploited to cut off parts of the system.
Behavioral Sensitivity/Fragility	Some dynamic resource allocations can have ranges with behavioral sensitivities.
Malleability	Dynamic allocation triggers could be manipulated with activity to move the system into less-desirable configurations.
Gullibility/Deceivability/ Naiveté	Dynamic allocations could be used to manipulate the system into less-desirable configurations.
Complacency	The existence of allocation plans may make one feel overly secure.
Corruptibility/ Controllability	Dynamic allocation control structures could be exploited.
Hard to Manage or Control	Dynamic allocations can be difficult to manage as options increase.
Self-Unawareness and Unpredictability	It may be hard to predict how the system will operate under different allocations. It may also be difficult to monitor the system status if the allocations are made automatically and rapidly.
Predictability	Even dynamic allocations can be predictable if the decision criteria are known.

Table A.32

Vulnerabilities That Can Be Incurred from General Management

Primary Cautions	
Centrality	Many management organizations have strong centralities.
Homogeneity	Highly managed organizations tend to be homogeneous and intolerant of alternative approaches, systems, and designs that introduce additional management costs and efforts.

Table A.32—Continued

Secondary Cautions	
Uniqueness	Key management functions can be placed with unique components or people.
Design Sensitivity/ Fragility/Limits/ Finiteness	Management controls can introduce limits and fragilities on capabilities.
Rigidity	Management systems can be rigid and hard to adapt to new situations.
Gullibility/Deceivability/ Naiveté	Rigid, highly structured management systems can be deceived when their processes are well understood by adversaries.
Complacency	Detailed management procedures can lead people to believe that the systems are sufficiently protected.
Predictability	Highly structured and micromanaged systems can follow well-known approaches. Documentation about these management structures can make it predictable if it is compromised.

Table A.33

Vulnerabilities That Can Be Incurred from Threat Response Structures and Plans

Primary Cautions	
Separability	Some response structures disconnect and partition the system in high-threat conditions to protect from attack.
Rigidity	Plans might be overly structured and rigid, especially if they apply broadly and do not account for local differences.
Gullibility/Deceivability/ Naiveté	Overly structured and rigid plans might be triggered to move the system into overly protective states, reducing capability at the low cost of tripping the triggers.
Secondary Cautions	
Centrality	Some response structures and plans employ centralized monitoring, decisionmaking, and implementation.
Homogeneity	Plans might dictate uniform responses across the board rather than allowing local differences.
Logic/Implementation Errors; Fallibility	Many plans have never been fully exercised in the real world and may contain unforeseen difficulties.
Design Sensitivity/Fragility/ Limits/Finiteness	Some response actions can limit performance as they seek to protect critical capabilities.
Behavioral Sensitivity/Fragility	Many plans have never been fully exercised in the real world and may contain unforeseen difficulties.
Complacency	The presence of contingency plans can lead to complacency unless they are often reexamined and expanded.
Accessible/Detectable/ Identifiable/Transparent/ Interceptable	If care is not taken, the actions taken in the plan can be quite visible and convey state information.
Self-Unawareness and Unpredictability	Many plans have never been fully exercised in the real world and may contain unforeseen difficulties.
Predictability	If well known, contingency plans can make it easier to predict how the system will react to threats and damage.

Table A.34

Vulnerabilities That Can Be Incurred from Rapid Reconstitution and Recovery

Secondary Caution	
Complacency	The ability to rapidly recover and reconstitute (e.g., reboot) the original system state can make us complacent about failures and compromises of the system and give us a false sense of operational capability.

Table A.35

Vulnerabilities That Can Be Incurred from Adaptability and Learning

Secondary Cautions	
Behavioral Sensitivity/Fragility	Adaptive exploration of parameters can temporarily introduce fragilities and degraded performance until they are well examined.
Malleability	Adaptation algorithms, if known, could be exploited to mislead the system.
Gullibility/Deceivability/ Naiveté	Adaptation algorithms, if known, could be exploited to mislead the system.
Hard to Manage or Control	If independent, adaptive systems can be harder to control.
Self-Unawareness and Unpredictability	Some adaptive algorithms are hard for humans to understand how they work.

Table A.36

Vulnerabilities That Can Be Incurred from Immunological Defense Systems

Secondary Cautions	
Centrality	Some immunological systems rely on centralized information and coordination sites. Decentralized, peer-to-peer architectures mitigate this.
Homogeneity	Since it is easier to apply this approach to homogeneous components, its application may drive management to more homogeneous configurations.
Malleability	The automatic update path provides a new means for broad manipulation across the information system components and must be highly protected.
Complacency	While valuable and seemingly robust, these systems are not perfect and must not lead to complacency in other security areas.
Corruptibility/ Controllability	The automatic update path provides a new means for broad corruptions across the information system components and must be highly protected.
Predictability	The sharing channel could introduce a means for adversary intelligence.

Table A.37

Vulnerabilities That Can Be Incurred from Vaccination

Secondary Cautions	
Homogeneity	Because it is easier to apply this approach to homogeneous components, its application may drive management to more homogeneous configurations.
Malevolence	One must be careful that simulated attacks do not introduce irreparable damage, introduce new problems, or make it easier for adversaries to understand how to attack the system.
Corruptibility/ Controllability	One must be careful that simulated attacks do not corrupt the system.
Predictability	One must be careful that simulated attacks do not make it easier for adversaries to understand how to attack the system.

Table A.38

Vulnerabilities That Can Be Incurred from Intelligence Operations

Secondary Cautions	
Centrality	Intelligence information flows are usually centralized to coordinate and exploit the information.
Separability	Intelligence activities can make individuals suspicious of each other.
Complacency	The existence of an intelligence capability can make us feel more secure than is warranted.

Table A.39

Vulnerabilities That Can Be Incurred from Self-Awareness, Monitoring, and Assessments

Secondary Cautions	
Centrality	Monitoring the entire system may require a centralized fusion and exploitation capability.
Complacency	Large amounts of indigestible information or long periods of false positives can make people indifferent.
Accessible/Detectable/ Identifiable/Transparent/ Interceptable	Our monitors might be exploited by our adversaries.

Table A.40

Vulnerabilities That Can Be Incurred from Deception for ISR

Secondary Cautions	
Centrality	Effective deceptions often require coordinated planning.
Hard to Manage or Control	Deceptions in our own systems can confuse our own managers if they are not identified.
Self-Unawareness and Unpredictability	Deceptions in our own systems can confuse our own managers and components if they are not identified.

Table A.41

Vulnerabilities That Can Be Incurred from Attack Detection, Recognition, Damage Assessment, and Forensics (Self and Foe)

Secondary Cautions	
Centrality	These assessments may require centralized information sources to facilitate fusion and other analyses.
Separability	Uncertain or faulty detections or conclusions can lead to internal suspicions, disconnections, and denials of information exchange.

Table A.42

Vulnerabilities That Can Be Incurred from General Counterintelligence

Secondary Cautions	
Separability	Excessive fears and alarms can make entities suspect one another, and lead to isolation.
Behavioral Sensitivity/Fragility	Excessive concerns about compromises and intrusions can make the system paranoid.
Gullibility/Deceivability/ Naiveté	Even counterintelligence efforts can be manipulated.
Hard to Manage or Control	Counterintelligence efforts can interfere with regular management functions and controls.

Table A.43

Vulnerabilities That Can Be Incurred from Unpredictable to Adversary

Primary Caution	
Self-Unawareness and Unpredictability	Unpredictability and complexities can confuse our own managers and components if they are not identified.
Secondary Cautions	
Separability	Excessive fears and alarms can make entities suspect one another and lead to isolation.
Behavioral Sensitivity/Fragility	Excessive concerns about compromises and intrusions can make the system paranoid.
Gullibility/Deceivability/ Naiveté	Even counterintelligence efforts can be manipulated.
Hard to Manage or Control	Counterintelligence efforts can interfere with regular management functions and controls.

Table A.44

Vulnerabilities That Can Be Incurred from Deception for CI

Primary Caution	
Self-Unawareness and Unpredictability	Deceptions can confuse our own managers and components if they are not identified.

Table A.44—Continued

Secondary Cautions	
Separability	Excessive deceptions can make it hard for entities to know what is real, leading to internal suspicions and isolations.
Behavioral Sensitivity/Fragility	Excessive deceptions can introduce behavioral anomalies when legitimate users are not aware of deceptions.
Hard to Manage or Control	Deceptions can interfere with regular management functions and controls.

Table A.45

Vulnerabilities That Can Be Incurred from Deterrence

Secondary Cautions	
Rigidity	Strong threats and penalties can make the system conservative, rigid, and cautious.
Complacency	Strong deterrence may naively make the system feel secure.
Predictability	Strong threats and penalties can make the system conservative, rigid, cautious, and thus predictable.

Table A.46

Vulnerabilities That Can Be Incurred from Criminal and Legal Penalties and Guarantees

Secondary Caution	
Complacency	Strong penalties and guarantees can introduce a false sense of security.

Table A.47

Vulnerabilities That Can Be Incurred from Law Enforcement; Civil Proceedings

Secondary Caution	
Complacency	Strong law enforcement can introduce a false sense of security.

BIBLIOGRAPHY

Alberts, Christopher, and Audrey Dorofee, *OCTAVE℠ Threat Profiles*, Pittsburgh, Pa.: Carnegie Mellon University, Software Engineering Institute, n.d., www.cert.org/archive/pdf/OCTAVEthreatProfiles.pdf (accessed June 2003).

Alberts, Christopher J., Sandra G. Behrens, Richard D. Pethia, and William R. Wilson, *Operationally Critical Threat, Asset, and Vulnerability Evaluation℠ (OCTAVE℠) Framework*, Version 1.0, Pittsburgh, Pa.: Carnegie Mellon University, Software Engineering Institute, CMU/SEI-99-TR-017, June 1999.

Alberts, Christopher J., Audrey J. Dorofee, and Julia H. Allen, *OCTAVE℠ Catalog of Practices*, Version 2.0, Pittsburgh, Pa.: Carnegie Mellon University, Software Engineering Institute, CMU/SEI-2001-TR-020, October, 2001.

Anderson, Robert H., Phillip M. Feldman, Scott Gerwehr, Brian K. Houghton, Richard Mesic, John Pinder, Jeff Rothenberg, and James R. Chiesa, *Securing the U.S. Defense Information Infrastructure: A Proposed Approach*, Santa Monica, Calif.: RAND Corporation, MR-993-OSD/NSA/DARPA, 1999.

Common Criteria, *Common Criteria for Information Technology Security Evaluation—Part 1: Introduction and General Model*, CCIMB-99-031, Version 2.1, August 1999a.

_______, *Common Criteria for Information Technology Security Evaluation—Part 2: Security Function Requirements*, CCIMB-99-032, Version 2.1, August 1999b.

_______, *Common Criteria for Information Technology Security Evaluation—Part 3: Security Assurance Requirements*, CCIMB-99-033, Version 2.1, August 1999c.

_______, *Common Criteria for Information Technology Security Evaluation: User Guide*, October 1999d.

_______, *Common Methodology for Information Technology Security Evaluation, Part 2: Evaluation Methodology*, CEM-99/045, Version 1.0, August 1999e.

Dutch Ministry of Transport, Public Works, and Water Management, and Dutch Ministry of Economic Affairs, *Internet Vulnerability*, July 2001, www.dgtp.nl/docs/intvul.pdf (accessed June 2003).

Gerwehr, Scott, and Russell W. Glenn, *The Art of Darkness: Deception and Urban Operations*, Santa Monica, Calif.: RAND Corporation, MR-1132-A, 2000.

Hamby, Zhi, "What the Heck Is OPSEC?" 2002, at the OPSEC Professionals Society webpage, www.opsec.org/who (accessed June 2003).

International Organization for Standardization (ISO), *Information Technology: Code of Practice for Information Security Management*, ISO/IEC 17799:2000(E), first edition, Geneva, Switzerland, December 1, 2000.

Joint Chiefs of Staff, *Command and Control for Joint Air Operations*, Joint Publication 3-56.1, November 14, 1994, www.adtdl.army.mil/cgi-bin/atdl.dll/jt/3-56_1/3-56_1 toc.htm (accessed June 2003).

_______, *Joint Doctrine for Operations Security*, Joint Publication 3-54, January 24, 1997.

_______, *DoD Dictionary of Military and Associated Terms*, Joint Publication 1-02, June 5, 2003 (last update), http://www.dtic.mil/doctrine/jel/doddict/.

Kent, Glenn A., and William E. Simons, "Objective-Based Planning," in Paul K. Davis, ed., *New Challenges for Defense Planning: Rethinking How Much Is Enough*, Santa Monica, Calif.: RAND Corporation, MR-400-RC, 1994, pp. 59–71.

Lewis, Leslie, and C. Robert Roll, *Strategy-to-Tasks: A Methodology for Resource Allocation and Management*, Santa Monica, Calif.: RAND Corporation, P-7839, 1993.

Minehart, Robert F., Jr., "Information Warfare Tutorial," Army War College, 1998, at http://carlisle-www.army.mil/usacsl/divisions/std/branches/iw/tutorial/intro.htm (accessed June 2003).

Thaler, David E., *Strategies to Tasks: A Framework for Linking Means and Ends*, Santa Monica, Calif.: RAND Corporation, MR-300-AF, 1993.

U.S. Army Communications Electronics Command, *OPSEC Primer*, Fort Monmouth, N.J.: Software Engineering Center (SEC) Security Office, June 27, 1999.

U.S. Department of the Air Force, "Operational Risk Management," Air Force Instruction 90-901, April 1, 2000a.

_______, "Operational Risk Management," Air Force Policy Directive 90-9, April 1, 2000b.

_______, "Operational Risk Management (ORM) Guidelines and Tools," Air Force Pamphlet 90-902, December 14, 2000c.

U.S. Department of the Army, Headquarters, *Army Regulation 530-1, Operations Security (OPSEC)*, Washington, D.C.: U.S. Government Printing Office, unclassified, distribution limited, March 3, 1995.

U.S. Naval Safety Center, "Operational Risk Management (ORM)," OPNAV Instruction 3500.39A/Marine Corps Order 3500.27A, July 1997.

_______, "Introduction to Operational Risk Management," Naval Safety Center, n.d., www.safetycenter.navy.mil/orm/generalorm/introduction/default.htm (accessed June 2003).

_______, "Operational Risk Management" (webpage), www.safetycenter.navy.mil/orm/default.htm (accessed June 2003).

Williams, Gary, "Operations Security (OPSEC)," Ft. Leavenworth, Kan.: Center for Army Lessons Learned, 1999, http://call.army.mil/products/trngqtr/tq3-99/opsec.htm (accessed June 2003).